CW01502190

Bac

Having been brought up in the small town of Frome, I had never come across controlled drugs or prostitution before. I knew my sister and her husband had tried both cannabis and LSD, but I had never seen any, let alone tried it. I'm sure there were prostitutes in Frome but none I knew of, and I was not aware of any gossip in the town about where the prostitutes hung out. I left school just short of my 18th birthday and by the age of 18 ½ I had joined the Avon and Somerset Police and was stationed at Broadbury Road police station in the heart of the infamous Knowle West council estate.

I noticed that it was not until the early 1980's that drugs started to appear on the estate. It was becoming more and more common to find drugs when searching cars, houses, or people. The drugs of choice then were the various forms of cannabis, like resin, weed, skunk and occasionally cannabis oil. The other drug that was often found was amphetamine. It was not until later that heroin and other drugs became more popular. I always found it terrible to see the harm that drugs did to people's lives, the individuals taking the drugs could be seen to physically deteriorate rapidly. The cost of drugs meant that families struggled to survive as all the available money was being spent on drugs due to the users' dependence on them. This gave me the desire to hunt down drugs dealers to take them off the streets. I knew there would always be someone else out there to replace the dealer, but it seemed right to prosecute those living off the suffering of others.

The Vice Squad is a section of the police force that deals with crime relating to drugs, pornography, prostitution, illegal sales of alcohol and gambling. I had never done vice squad work and my involvement in vice matters developed over many years working in district CID offices. I learnt about drugs offences and prostitution offences from my more experienced colleagues, and the only reason that I grew to be quite experienced and knowledgeable was because of them.

I would make a special mention of one uniform Acting Sergeant and two Detective Constables that I worked with during my years at Trinity Road, St George and Staplehill police stations.

Malcolm Cobb was a very experienced police constable who had worked many years in the inner city and at the time I met him, he was an acting sergeant at Trinity Road police district. He introduced me to the world of prostitution and illegal drinking dens that operated within the St Pauls area. I learnt how to police this type of offence in a positive yet constructive way. I spent twelve months policing St Pauls and acquired a fascinating insight into the vice scene.

Paul Hopes was only 3 years older than me, and he joined my CID office in St George having completed many years on the Force

Drugs Squad. Paul still preferred to deal with drugs related offences and would opt to do that rather than some of the more menial district CID work. He was extremely good at recruiting informants and would get information about significant major criminals and their activities. I was Paul's supervisor so was often called upon to set up operations to support the information that Paul had obtained. I gained a vast amount of knowledge from him in how to plan drugs surveillance operations.

Ian Hieron (Himey) was 7 years younger than me; he was extremely enthusiastic and keen to deal with any and everything that came his way. I would guess that he was the best thief taker in the department because he knew everyone in the area we policed. He had grown up and gone to school in Oldland Common so knew the area and people well. Ian was another one who was always getting information and cultivated many informants. I was fortunate to work alongside Himey and deal with several informants with him, learning quickly that they could never be trusted but also how useful they were as a source of information that could get quick results on crimes committed and even on occasions, preventing the crime before or as it was happening. Meeting and paying informants became second nature to me thanks to both Paul and Himey.

Drugs

Chapter 1:

Shatiff

In 1995, I was a Detective Sergeant at St George police station and Paul Hopes was looking at the activities of a drug dealer called Javid Shatiff (Pseudonym). To make things easier I will refer to him by his family name Shatiff.

Shatiff was an Asian male aged 29 years who lived in a large four bedroomed detached property in North Common with his girlfriend. He drove around in a large smart black Lexus motor car.

We had become aware of him dealing heroin in Bristol and Paul had asked that he be allowed to investigate Shatiff's drugs dealing activities. Paul had sent feelers out for any information and early in May 1995, he received a telephone call from the West Midlands Crime

Squad who wished to meet us to discuss some new information they had about Shatiff.

We met up in the car park of the Crest Hotel, Hambrook, on the outskirts of Bristol and they informed us that they had recently been approached by an informant from Birmingham, who could supply details about Shatiff's drug dealing activities. The informant (Mr C) was a small-time drug user who had been buying small quantities of heroin from an unnamed man in Birmingham. Mr C's supplier, in turn, would frequently travel to Bristol to purchase his heroin in large quantities from Shatiff. The reason the informant came forward with information was because Shatiff had upped the stakes and insisted that he would only sell heroin in amounts of £5,000 minimum. This in turn had resulted in the prices going up in Birmingham so Mr C was not happy with Shatiff. The informant wanted to teach Shatiff a lesson so had gone straight to the police. No honour amongst criminals. The information that he was able to give was when his supplier was next travelling to Bristol to score £5000+ of heroin from Shatiff. The informant knew times and places that the exchange of money and drugs would take place.

The Crime Squad had suggested we meet in the Crest hotel car park on the outskirts of Bristol to discuss the information with us. The location was handy for them travelling from Birmingham as it was just off the motorway. We met on the 10th of May, and it was only once we had obtained the full story that I understood why they had chosen to meet us at that location. The informant had told them that at about 2pm on the following Wednesday 17th May, Shatiff had planned to meet the Birmingham dealer in the car park of the Crest hotel, and it would be there, that the heroin would be exchanged for cash, the exact amounts was not known but the informant assumed it had to be at least £5000 worth. The deal would only take a few minutes and Shatiff would then take his money to his Bristol address and hide it in the attic there. The informant did not know where Shatiff lived but we already had that information.

We had one week to work out how to overcome the problem of getting many officers, unnoticed, in the car park of the Crest Hotel. They would need to be close enough to be able to pounce on Shatiff without giving him the opportunity to dispose of the evidence.

Paul and I hatched a plan where Paul would be sat with a WPC Caroline Walters in his own car, close to the entrance of the hotel car park so he could see any cars and occupants approaching. They would be a courting couple to anyone seeing them (This was close to the truth in any case as they both got married one year later). I would then have a small team of five officers dressed as gardeners. Between us, we managed to drum up various items of garden tools and even had suitable clothing to wear. I looked like the head gardener. I was wearing blue overalls, a blue tatty wax jacket, boots and a flat cap. Unlike most gardeners, we were all wearing hats to conceal earphones which we needed to communicate as a group.

At midday we received a call from the West Midlands Crime Squad to confirm that the deal was still to take place as the dealer from Birmingham was on his way and the exchange was still planned at about 2pm. We didn't want to spend too much time as gardeners in the car park so we arrived at 1:30pm. The management at the Crest Hotel had been most helpful and agreed to us using their grounds for the sting. They even suggested what gardening was required.

We were all in position, checked our covert radios which consisted of wireless earphones so there were no wires showing and a transmitter button which was hidden within our gloves. There was nothing else to do but wait so we started gardening. There were a lot of rotting leaves on the flower borders and several of the trees and bushes seemed overgrown. Raking up the leaves and taking them to a newly formed compost heap seemed like a good idea and we also chose to do some pruning.

In previous deals involving Shatiff, he had been accompanied by a 'bodyguard' so we needed to stay alert and be prepared for a degree of violence.

The best-laid plans always have their problems, the Birmingham target (Target 1) did not arrive on site until 4:40pm! He appeared to be on the phone as he arrived in the carpark and later phone billings showed he made a call to Shatiff. He parked in the corner of zone 3 and sat waiting.

The leaf clearing was nearly complete and the trees were looking quite small by now. Luckily the hotel gardener had arrived earlier and pointed out to us that the rotting leaves were in fact mulch and deliberately on the flowerbeds to prevent weeds growing! We then started the job of returning the mulch to the flowerbeds.

The time was now 5pm and we were ready for whatever was thrown at us. The Birmingham target was sat in his car in the corner of the car park so we stayed well clear of that area. It was then that I heard the call through my earphones:

"Possible target on plot. One white male shaven head in Nissan motor vehicle B123 DEF". (Target2)

Nothing like the black Lexus we hoped would turn up. The car and driver were known to us, but it was a little disappointing that Shatiff was not present in the car. Was this a dry run? Did the car's occupant have any drugs with him? What should we do? These were all questions going through my mind at this point. It would be a shame to move in and find out that Shatiff was about to turn up a few minutes later. I decided that we would stand off and let the two targets meet up and exchange goods and then pounce immediately, catching them both in the act of being concerned in the supply of drugs.

"Target 2 turning left into parking zone two, Standby".

We had divided the car park into zones so everyone would know where we were talking about. I was still pruning bushes at this point but was slowly moving closer and closer as it was now my responsibility to take over commentary and call the strike. I had to cover both zone 2 and zone 3 as we had no idea where the two parties would meet up.

"Gary to all units, I have eyeball, standby".

A coach arrived and parked near the car park entrance and then a large number of people walked from the hotel towards the coach. I didn't recognise them, but they were the Rovers football team getting on a coach to head out to Wembley. There were TV cameras filming as well. All we needed!

"Target 2 now parked up in zone 2, standby".

The two vehicles were now located in separate zones of the car park but the deal was looking more and more likely it was going to take place in zone 2 near to where Target 2 had parked

"Target 1 is now approaching Target 2's vehicle, standby".

I could see all my fellow gardeners slowly moving into position to be able to move in from all directions.

"Target 2 still in driver's seat but now talking to Target 1 who is stood alongside vehicle, Standby".

All going to plan, they simply had to exchange drugs for money.

We had a contingency plan for Paul to use his vehicle to prevent an escape if necessary but as it was Paul's own car that was a last resort.

"Target 2 vehicle is still stationary, Target 1 now walking away, nothing has exchanged between them, standby".

My heart was beating fast, lots of thoughts going through my mind. I had been close enough and could be sure nothing had passed between the two and I knew no exchange had yet taken place.

I could strike now and hopefully catch Target 2 with the drugs or wait in a hope that Target 1 would return with the money to make the purchase. Both targets appeared on edge and I couldn't take the chance that they had called it all off and would now both drive off. The two targets were some distance apart by now and Target 1 was getting near to his parked car. I made my decision that we needed to pounce; I was sure the drugs were still with the driver of the Nissan so he had to be our primary target with the heroin. We had recognised him as one of our local drugs users and associate of Shatiff called Anthony Archer. I shouted those immortal words.

"All units Strike, Strike, Strike."

It was quite impressive to see gardeners from all directions pouncing on the target vehicle and dragging the young lad from the car. I retrieved £5,000 worth of heroin tucked into the waistband of his trousers. As Archer was being hand cuffed, I could see the cameraman filming the whole incident and had to point out to him that the film could not be shown on television until after any court case.

Target 2 was pursued on foot by two of our team but unfortunately he had been too close to his car when the strike was called, he jumped in and drove off at speed directly towards Paul's vehicle, he bounced up over the verge and was gone. We put out observations for the car on the motorway heading back to Birmingham, but it was found abandoned later that evening.

The informant Mr C told the Crime Squad that the money returned to Birmingham and more heroin was purchased a week later from Shatiff at a different location. I am aware that Mr C received £75 for the information he supplied regarding Shatiff and I am fairly certain I know what he spent the money on.

At least we had recovered £5,000 worth Shatiff's drugs and his runner was in custody.

Anthony Archer was convicted of possessing a controlled drug with intent to supply and got 2 years imprisonment. He believed that Shatiff had set him up but because he was too afraid of Shatiff he would not tell us who was behind the drug deal. Shatiff remained a police target, but it was the Crime Squad that took him on.

The phone call between Archer and Shatiff was not enough evidence to justify an arrest, but he would come another day.

Chapter 2:

The Money

It was Monday 14th April 2003 and like any normal Monday morning in the Staplehill CID office, I was trying to catch up with the weekend's events to see if there were any new investigations to allocate. Things had been quiet and we were approaching the Easter break when I was due a week off from Good Friday the 18th.

I heard the phone ringing and it was quickly answered by someone from my team in the adjacent office. Within ten minutes, I discovered that DC Andy Hailes had taken the call as he popped his head into my office to let me know what it was all about. The control room reported that a local builder, David Peters had phoned to say that whilst he was working alone in a house in Staplehill, he had reason to go into the attic and had discovered a holdall full of used bank notes and he wanted the police to attend because he didn't wish to be accused of theft should any of the money go missing. The first thing that went through my mind was why the control room had requested CID attendance rather than a uniform officer. Was this some form of integrity test being carried out by the Force Professional Standards Department to see if all the money were correctly seized and recorded in the detained property store. I told Andy that I would go with him so we could corroborate each other regarding the money.

We arrived at the three bedroomed semi-detached property and were invited into the house by Mr Peters. The house was clearly not lived in with all the rooms being bare of furniture. David Peters explained that the owner and landlord of the property was a man called Javid Shatiff and he was looking to refurbish the whole house before renting it out again or selling it. Mr Peters had frequently carried out building works on Mr Shatiff's properties and he was aware that the previous tenants of this house had vacated the property two months earlier. A substantial amount of work had to be done by Mr Peters and he had been supplied with a house key in order to gain entry to the house whenever he needed.   Mr Peters had been working at the house for about six weeks and it was at about 10:00am that morning that he had gone for the first time into the attic to gain access above the bedroom ceiling to carry out some repair work. Mr Peters had seen a large black holdall behind the chimney stack and as it was the only thing in the loft he decided to look inside.   He guessed that there was about £100,000 in used bank notes in the bag so decided to phone the police.   He had been unable to make phone contact with Mr Shatiff and when he had phoned Shatiff's friend, he had been told that Javid was out of the country on business.   Mr Peters then took us into the kitchen to show us the holdall.

The bag was a large Adidas holdall about 30cm x 35cm x 65cm and was full to the top with Bank of England notes. I had no idea of the quantity of money but knew that I had never come across such a large amount in one place before. Andy and I had arrived at the house with a number of large plastic bags and several tamper proof seals as we knew that if we were going to seize the money, we would seal it in bags with numbered seals so there was never any suggestion of money going missing. Mr Peters took a phone call on his mobile and then handed me the phone saying that the caller wished to talk to me. The caller claimed to be a business associate of Javid Shatiff and he stated that he was heading around to the house as he wished to be present to see what was being seized. He claimed to be only five minutes away so I agreed to await his arrival.

I saw the black BMW as it pulled up on the opposite side of the road, about six houses down towards Frenchay. There was plenty of parking immediately outside the house so I was already suspicious before I even met the man. I made a note of the BMW's index number and watched as two men dressed in smart suits approached the house. The men introduced themselves and provided proof of their identities before I allowed them into the house. Both were white men in their 40's, smartly dressed and well spoken. It once again entered my mind that they could be undercover police officers testing our honesty.

Through conversations with the men, I was able to confirm that Javid Shatiff was the person who I believed it to be, namely Javid Shatiff a well-known drugs dealer. We checked around the house and Andy checked the attic and we were satisfied that there was nothing else suspicious concealed. I told the men that I would be seizing all the money and would return it to Mr Shatiff if he could prove he had lawful possession of it. I told the men that I would be leaving a receipt to confirm what had been seized and they were welcome to sign it as witnesses. The men insisted that the money be counted before it left the house as they were not happy that a numbered sealed bag was suitable. I explained that I had no intention on spending hours counting out the large sum of money and that the sealed bags would not be unsealed until Mr Shatiff had seen them. Although they were not happy, the money was placed in three separate numbered sealed bags and the holdall was also taken. A receipt was left at the house and Andy and I drove the five minutes back to the station where we placed the sealed bags in the police station safe.

Mr Shatiff was due back from holiday in two weeks which tied in well with my return from the Easter break. There was only so much we could do at this stage until we knew what Javid Shatiff had to say about the money. We tracked down the ex-tenants of the house and they explained that they had lived in the house for two years, paying rent to Mr Shatiff. They considered him a good landlord and it was them who chose to leave the address as they were hoping to purchase a house. They had vacated the premises on 31st January and left none of their own property behind. The house had been rented as furnished so all the furniture and kitchen appliances were the property of Mr Shatiff. They were aware that Mr Shatiff had decided to refurbish the whole house before selling it on. The ex-tenants had only been up into the loft on about four occasions during the two years they occupied the house and even then, they only poked their heads through the hatch to reach their cases that they stored near the entrance. As far as they could recall, the attic was empty and they had no idea of any holdall or money. They provided us with their fingerprints for elimination purposes.

We had no intention of breaking the seals on the plastic bags containing the money until we had shown the cash to Shatiff, but we were able to submit the holdall for fingerprinting. There was nothing else about the holdall that made it unique and no enquiries we could make about where or when it had been purchased.

Enquiries were made into the two men who called at the house when we were seizing the cash. I was pleased to see that they were not undercover police officers. They were both joint owners of a local gym used by the criminal fraternity as a place to hang out. They had a very limited criminal history, just convictions for making threats, assault and criminal damage. There was no intelligence to show any links with drugs.

It was not until Thursday the 8th of May that Shatiff finally turned up at Staplehill Police station by appointment to be interviewed about the money recovered from his house. Shatiff had been asked to bring with him any proof of his legal ownership of the money. He arrived with a legal advisor by his side who was there to ensure that he didn't incriminate himself.

Before I continue with the story, I should point out that the police had a mass of intelligence that Shatiff was a significant heroin dealer but he had only been convicted once for supplying heroin and that related to a moderate amount and nothing like the quantity that intelligence suggested he was dealing in. He was known to make his money on properties that he owned and rented as well as having a stake in the same local gym.

Shatiff was clearly hoping to have his money back and he went on to give his account of where the money came from and why it was in the attic of a void house. Shatiff agreed that the property in Staplehill was his and that it was currently being repaired and decorated before he put it up for sale. He liked to buy, rent and sell property as a means of income. He was able to produce paperwork to prove his ownership of the house. With regards to the money, he stated that it was his money and it was for use in another business enterprise he was hoping to set up. He was intending to go into business with his uncle and two other un-named associates in the cigarette manufacturing industry. He had been tasked by them to make enquiries about purchasing an industrial cigarette making machine for use in the business. The money recovered from the attic was the money to be used for that purchase. He then produced two letters purporting to be from companies in India that were both agreements in principle to the purchase of cigarette making machines at a price of about £50,000 each. The two letters looked official and were on headed paper, both dated in January 2003. He explained that the letters were proof of his intention to purchase machinery and since January, he had been gathering together the finances to complete the deal. He only intended to purchase one machine at this time and had not committed to either of the machines referred to in the letters. Shatiff stated that the money in the holdall was monies he had collected from his uncle, the other two associates and his money that he had amassed from calling in debts. He would not expand on the nature of the debts that he had collected on the advice of his solicitor. When asked how much money was in the holdall, Shatiff stated about £62,000. We showed him the recovered money and holdall and he agreed that it was his. When asked why he had chosen to store that amount of cash in the attic of an unalarmed void house, he said that he did not like using banks and didn't trust them. When asked how long the money had been in the attic, he said he had put it there early in February about a week after his tenants had moved out. I asked why he had not stored the cash in his own home, which was occupied and alarmed and therefore more secure. He responded *"I have my reasons"* but would not explain any more. Although he supplied his uncle's details, he would not give the names of the other two people allegedly involved in the business venture. The only other document Shatiff supplied was a typed letter which appeared to be from his uncle giving Shatiff authority to purchase a cigarette making machine on his behalf.

I explained to Shatiff that I would be making extensive enquiries into his explanation for the recovered money and that I would no doubt have further questions to ask him once those enquiries were complete. I explained that it was our intention to go to a bank and use their money counting facilities to establish exactly how much money was in the holdall and he agreed with that. I pointed out that when such large sums of money are found concealed as in this case, we had to rule out that it was not the proceeds of crime such as drugs supply, bearing in mind he did have a previous conviction for such an offence. Before leaving the station Shatiff asked that we make our enquiries as quick as possible as he wished to have his money back.

Folded bundles of cash

Andy Hailes and I took the money to a large bank in Whiteladies Road in Bristol where we broke the numbered seals in order to look at the money and to use the bank's counting machine. The grand total proved to be £98,790. It was during this counting process that we noticed that large bundles of the money were unusually folded in a way often associated with drugs dealers.

We decided to take sample notes from a few of these bundles in order to submit for forensic testing. It was recognised, at the time, that around 80% of all British banknotes contain traces of drugs but higher levels of contaminants were the result of either being handled by people using drugs or dealing in drugs. The concentration levels of contaminants had been used as evidence in past court cases against drug dealers when the levels proved greater than normal notes in general circulation. We wanted to establish if there was evidence that these recovered notes were contaminated more than normal indicating that the notes could be connected to the supply of drugs rather than the explanation given by Shatiff.

The forensic test used was known as tandem mass-spectrometry and our results, although a slightly higher level of drugs was found on the bank notes than you may expect for notes in general circulation, they were not high enough to be conclusive evidence of money connected to drugs supply.

Amongst the recovered money were many bank note bands to keep bundles together but none of these contained any information regarding the source. There were also a number of bundles containing notes with consecutive numbers, possibly suggesting new notes withdrawn from cashpoint machines. We confirmed that the notes were all genuine currency. Counterfeit currency was in circulation in Bristol at the time and was regularly turning up in local stores.

Shatiff's uncle confirmed that he had discussed with his nephew the possibility of purchasing a cigarette making machine and to go into business together but had no idea how much progress had been made. He had no idea of any other associate or business partner and had not handed over any money. He could not recall supplying a letter but would not rule out the possibility that he had. Enquiries were made of the two companies in India whose headed note paper had been used but they had no record of sending any correspondence to Shatiff, they both accepted the headed letters were similar to those they used and they confirmed that they do sell cigarette making machines from time to time. In one case, the name on the signed letter was not even an employee of the company so they believed it to be false. It looked very much like Shatiff had identified companies in India and had faked letters by creating headed paper similar to the companies own to support his cover story.

Shatiff was called in to Staplehill police station for further interview and he was again accompanied by his legal advisor. We first told him that there had been £98,970 in the holdall and not the £62,000 that he had referred to in his initial interview. He explained that he had guessed the total and had no idea of the precise amount in the holdall. Having gathered the money together he would often borrow from the holdall and return money as he needed it. He accepted that he was way out on his estimate. Shatiff insisted that the two typed letters from the companies in India were genuine and it was their poor record keeping that was the reason for any confusion. He insisted that he had collected some money from his uncle, although he could not say how much but suggested his uncle was confused or just mistaken if he had denied handing any over. He could not even say how much of his other two business associates had supplied him to date either. I explained that I found it difficult to accept that he had no idea who had supplied what money towards the funds as how would he know who had contributed what to their new venture. Shatiff simply explained that the whole arrangement was quite loose but everyone was happy with it. Shatiff could offer no explanation as to the various ways the money was bundled up, it was just how he had received it and the money had come from many people over a long period of time. He had been happy to accept it in any way it was given to him.

I informed Shatiff that my enquiries were still not complete and his money would be retained by the police until the investigation was finalised. The money was to be placed in an account that would gain interest as was standard procedure to avoid any claims of loss of interest while the police were in possession of the money.

It was about six months later that an officer from the Force Financial Investigations Unit made contact with me. He had been asked by the Force Crime Squad to look into Shatiff's financial affairs as they had a drugs supply case against him and would be looking to seize his assets under the Proceeds of Crime Act 2003. This was quite fortunate because the Crown Prosecution Service had decided that there was not enough evidence to take Shatiff to court on the possession of the money alone and we were considering handing him the money back along with any interest earned.

I was later to give evidence at Bristol Crown Court regarding the money found in Shatiff's property in Staplehill and it was all seized by the courts under the Proceeds of Crime Act. Result!

Chapter 3:

Styles and Wells

Like all districts, we had our fair share of high-level criminals and within that group were drugs dealers. We all knew who they were but so many warrants at their home addresses proved negative because the timing of the searches were wrong, or their hiding places were too good. This is where the informants could help. They would know when the dealers had a new stash of drugs, when and where they were selling the drugs from and often the latest hiding place. We could then time our search warrants and improve our chances of a successful find.

The second case I wish to write about involves two of our more active drugs dealers. I will refer to them by aliases as I have no idea if they are still in the business of supplying drugs or if they have cleaned up their acts. They deserve their privacy and anonymity if they have moved on. If they are still supplying drugs, I have no wish to advertise their business for them.

I will refer to them as Jimmy Styles and Troy Wells.

Jimmy was 10 years older than me, but he had led a life of crime. His crimes ranged from burglary, armed robbery, assaults, theft, fraud, and drugs supply. He could be quite violent and not someone to upset. He lived with his partner in a council house in the Fishponds area of Bristol. At any one time, there would be up to six other people staying at his house, these were people on the run from the police or courts, drugs users or people that Jimmy would use to run his drugs about for him to avoid being caught himself. Jimmy was very careful to avoid being in direct possession of any great quantity of drugs and his lodgers were always there to take the rap for Jimmy if necessary. He was one of the main heroin suppliers in that part of town. I wouldn't say he was uncatchable, but it would take a lot of planning to build a strong case.

Troy, on the other hand, lived with his common law wife and children in a council house in Warmley. His house was always being searched and the warrants were nearly always positive, but the results were poor. Small quantities of drugs and a few stolen goods of minimal value. He was more of a petty thief, shoplifter, burglar, and car thief. He was the area supplier of cannabis and smaller supplier of heroin but was not in competition with Jimmy.

Jimmy and Troy knew each other and would help each other out. Troy would purchase his heroin from Jimmy and do some running around to pay off debts. I would not describe them as friends, but they seem to understand how they could help each other out.

It was Paul Hopes who approached me one day as he had received new information about the activities of Jimmy Styles. Jimmy had recently moved to a new address in Fishponds and had arranged for a large consignment of heroin to come from a contact in London. Jimmy was intending to deal from his home to his regular customers as he did not believe the new house was known by the police. The precise date of the heroin arriving was not yet known but Paul had tasked his informant to find out. The informant was also pressed for information about where the drugs may be concealed in the house but as Jimmy had not lived there long, that information was not yet known.

I discussed with Paul how we could best get the evidence of drug supply as simply searching the address after being told the drugs had been collected may result in evidence of possession only. I also wanted to avoid the usual problem of someone else in the Styles household claiming to be the owner of any drugs found. The informant would need to be further tasked with finding out who else was currently living with Jimmy and his partner.

Paul who had already had experience of this type of investigation suggested a period of covert surveillance on the house, which would confirm that Jimmy was living at the address. We would also find out who else was staying there and would be able to monitor the drug users calling to purchase their drugs. We were quietly confident that we could visually identify several of the drug user visitors.

There was already current intelligence held on Jimmy Styles about the unregistered mobile phone that he was using for his drug dealing and this number was confirmed by Paul's informant.

It was not long before Paul had identified a suitable premises that could be used as an OP (Observation Point). I had to visit the premises to confirm that it was suitable and to record the owner's views, should the OP details be released in court. I would, if necessary, give evidence in court, without disclosing the location we used.

General district CID work continued, and it was necessary to fit in any surveillance as and when other commitments allowed.

Phase one of Operation Falcon was to simply observe and record what was seen. Special surveillance logs were used to record everything. I carried out duties in the OP on four occasions to fully understand how the OP worked. As it was the first time that I had used surveillance logs, I wanted to know how much detail had to be recorded of people visiting the target premises. Paul was able to instruct me on how to use them. I needed to satisfy myself that it would be possible to gain access and leave the OP undetected.

It was after 6 weeks of periodic surveillance that I agreed it was time to move to phase two. This would entail watching the target premises and hopefully identifying occasions when Jimmy was alone at home. We would then monitor callers who appeared to be drugs users, this proved easier that you might imagine. The callers we were interested in would often not even enter the house, staying at the door for a minute or two and then leaving. You could never see drugs changing hands, but you could see something being exchanged and the whole transaction would last about a minute. The plan was for officers to be in plain clothes in the vicinity to respond to calls from the OP. They would then follow the caller once they left the premises and when they were several streets away, the caller would be stopped and detained for a drugs search. The caller would be taken off the street to the nearby police station for a strip search. We were looking to reduce the chances of the operation being rumbled.

It was on the 23rd of January 1996, two police officers from the district intelligence unit were sat in the OP and monitoring the target address. I was sat in an unmarked police vehicle with Paul Hopes awaiting any radio messages from the OP to stop and detain callers to the target address. The time was 7:15pm and the police radio came to life:

"We've got a white male aged early twenties at the address. Target 1 (Styles) answered the door and has gone inside. The white male is waiting at the door".

About 2 minutes later the call came:

"The white male is leaving the address having taken possession of something from

Target 1, he is walking away in the direction of the city centre and looking at something in his right hand".

We were given a detailed description of this youth and soon had him in our sights. I agreed with Paul that he would be a good person to detain for a drugs search, so we followed him a short distance and once we were happy that we had gone far enough we approached him. The youth was Anthony Archer, who I had previously dealt with as Shatiff's runner. Paul and I introduced ourselves to him and told him that we believed that he may be in possession of controlled drugs, so we were detaining him for the purpose of carrying out a drugs search.

I said: *"Do you have any drugs on you".*

Anthony replied *"No".*

We were beginning to worry that this was going to be a negative search and could risk blowing the whole operation. Archer was taken in our police car to Staple Hill police station. Paul sat in the back of the car with Archer to make sure he was unable to dispose of any drugs en-route to the station. Once at Staplehill, we went into the holding area to carry out the search.

I had learnt from Paul that when carrying out a search, two officers should be present, one to carry out the search and the second to observe. Drugs users were very adept at finding the opportunity to discard their drugs when a searching officer was busy checking clothing or bags.

Archer was asked to remove his Jacket and Paul, wearing gloves, started to search the pockets and lining for anything concealed. I saw Paul remove a small wrap of paper from Archer's right jacket pocket and when the wrap was opened, it was clear that it contained brown powder. This was seized as an exhibit by Paul as possible controlled drugs. Heroin being the most likely due to the appearance of the powder.

Paul said to Archer: *"What is in this wrap?"*.

Archer replied *"Heroin"*.

Archer was then arrested on suspicion of possession of a controlled drug, and he made no reply after caution. The search continued but nothing further was found. Nothing was found at his home address either.

When interviewed with his solicitor present, Archer admitted the offence of possession of heroin for his own use and stated that he had bought it from an unknown person not long before he was stopped by the police. We were not too interested in prosecuting him for minor possession offences, so it was decided after checking on Archer's offending history that he would be suitable for an official caution.

It would not be the first time that drugs suppliers had conned the purchasers into buying what they believed to be drugs only to find the item was not drugs at all. We needed to test the brown powder to confirm if it was heroin before we cautioned Archer and before we were happy that we had our first bit of evidence towards forming a case against Styles for supply of controlled drugs. The test proved positive, and Archer was cautioned. He said goodbye to his solicitor, and we agreed to take him home.

It was now that Paul's other skills came into use. With no fear of prosecution held over him Archer, was persuaded to make a statement about when, where and from whom he had bought the drugs. He included how much he had paid and how he contacted his supplier on the phone. We knew that with Archer's phone number and Styles' phone number we could get further evidence. Operation Falcon was now properly under way. We knew there was a risk that Archer could tell Styles what he had done but with Styles' reputation of violence, we thought it unlikely.

The other evidence we had was the drugs, which was heroin cut with various other chemicals that may be unique to the batch being sold by Styles. The wrap was made from pages of a magazine and that might prove useful. We also had the possibility of fingerprints being recovered from the paper.

During the next few months, we carried out several similar stops and searches from visitors at the target address and each time the callers were found in possession of heroin and cautioned. Most gave statements or an account of where the drugs came from.

I will run through two more occasions that were of specific interest.

I was working once again with DC Hopes sat in an unmarked car in the vicinity of the target premises. It was 10pm on 30th of January and Paul and I were now quite used to responding to the OP calls. The call came two hours after we had first parked up on plot and we were getting a little impatient as midnight was the end of our shift.

"White male appears to have exchanged something with Target 1 at the address. He has now left and got into the driver's seat of a Blue Ford Granada B321LMN. Only one occupant. The car is leaving in the direction of Staplehill."

I instantly recognised the number of the Granada and knew that it was used by Troy Wells another local cannabis dealer. If he was visiting Styles, then it was almost certainly to do with drugs. We were soon on the tail of the Granada and with the help of uniform officers in a marked car we caused the Granada to pull over. It was as expected Troy driving the car. We had no real need to introduce ourselves because we had both arrested him before and searched his home many times for drugs and stolen goods.

I immediately went into my usual spiel:

"Troy, I have reason to believe you may be in possession of controlled drugs, so I am

detaining you for a drugs search. Do you have any drugs in your possession or in the car?"

He replied *"No".*

I wouldn't have expected any other reply from him. I took Wells to our police car and sat in the back with him, I was holding his arms out in front of him to prevent him from destroying evidence. He had previously been known to eat his drugs rather than be caught with them. We headed back towards Staplehill and one of the uniformed officers drove Wells' car back to the station for searching.

I would estimate we were about halfway back when Wells started to struggle, trying to break free from my grip on his arms. I had to be a little more forceful holding him down until one of the officers following us, climbed into the rear of our police car, and assisted in restraining Wells for the rest of the journey. One good thing about Wells' reaction was that it indicated that he may well have drugs in his possession.

As we arrived in the station yard Wells said:
"You'll find it when you search me so I might as well tell you now, it's in my trousers".

Wells arched his back, and I could see a plastic bag sticking out from the waistband of his trousers. I removed the self-seal bag, and it clearly contained a quantity of brown powder within it. I then arrested Wells on suspicion of possessing a controlled drug. He made no reply after caution. No more drugs were found in his car or in his home, but the quantity found in the bag was more substantial than for an offence of simple possession. Wells was interviewed in relation to possession of heroin with intent to supply and we seized his mobile phone to examine it for evidence and to link him to Styles. The powder was confirmed as heroin and Wells was released on bail for a decision to be made on charging.

We had reached the day for the final phase of operation Falcon. We planned to maintain observations once again on the target premises and on this occasion, we would identify a caller, detain them and assuming they were in possession of drugs we would execute a search warrant on Styles' home. We had used the evidence gathered during the previous arrests of the visitors for possession and the Magistrate had quite happily given us a search warrant for Styles home.

At 6:30pm on 7th March 1996, DC Hopes and I were parked up in our usual spot and the call came through from the OP:

"We have a white male caller to the address, and he appears to be making a purchase from Target 1. He is mid-twenties slim, wearing a black beany hat, red t-shirt, and jeans. Now walking away towards Staplehill."

We caught up with him and stopped him three streets away. Paul and I both knew him as Dave Marsh, a drug user and told him he was being detained for a drugs search. He immediately became aggressive, and it took both of us to restrain him by using arm locks and placing him over the bonnet of the police car. There was no way he would calm down sufficiently enough, so we requested the assistance of uniform officers. We needed to do a cursory search on the street to make sure he had no weapons that could cause us harm for the transport back to the station. I searched his right-hand jacket pocket where I found a packet of cigarettes. I could see that the box, as well as containing cigarettes contained three paper wraps and two torn pieces of paper bearing phone numbers. One of the phone numbers we recognised as Styles' burner phone.

Marsh was told that he was being arrested on suspicion of possession of controlled drugs and after he was cautioned, he replied:

"It's only personal, why don't you just give it back and say you didn't find it".

We did not like that suggestion and he was taken into the custody area and detained for interview. Dave made a no comment interview, but we had his paper wraps, the drugs, his phone, and the phone numbers to add to our list of evidence. Before he was bailed, his home was searched but we found nothing. We then set about executing the search warrant at the target premises.

For the target premises we had specially trained search officers from a support group assisted by five detectives including Paul and me. I had decided that we would not knock on the door so I authorised a forced entry to the house as we needed to gain entry quickly to surprise the occupants. Officers in the OP had already told us to expect at least six people in the house, Jimmy Styles, his partner, three unidentified males and an unidentified female. The front door unusually had a reinforced metal frame fitted to it, but the support group were well used to these tactics, and we were inside in seconds. The six occupants were arrested for conspiracy to supply controlled drugs and were all placed in handcuffs to prevent them from interfering with the search.

I handed Styles a copy of the search warrant and all those arrested, other than Styles' partner, were taken away to the police station. We only wanted one person present during the search, so we had full control of the scene. The search took many hours, we seized thirty wraps, drugs scales, money, mobile phones and cut up pieces of magazines.

The search in the house seemed thorough enough and had included searching a built-in larder, which had been converted into a chinchilla cage. I didn't realise that chinchilla have the habit of spitting at you when they get annoyed but that's obviously what happens! The two creatures were not at all happy having their home searched by the police and they ignored the fact that we had a warrant for the main house. What a good place it might have been to hide drugs.

We then moved to a search of the garden and shed which proved negative. Just before we were about to leave, one of the support group officers shouted:

"Kick it back to me Sarge".

I looked across as he kicked a football in my direction but instead of the ball rolling over to me, it stopped suddenly, and the officer started to cuss and hop about on one foot. An examination of the football showed it had a slit down the seam and inside in a carrier bag was an automatic handgun.

Football in garden

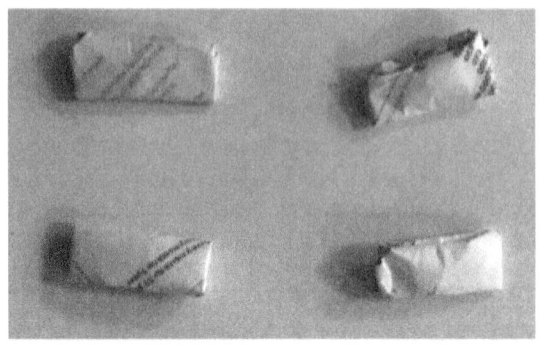

Typical drugs wraps

It became obvious that it was only Jimmy Styles, and his partner that were involved in the drugs supply and the others in the house were drugs users or Jimmy's runners, but we had no evidence against them.

Fingerprint evidence on one wrap seized from a caller to the target address was identified as belonging to Jimmy Styles. There was even a physical match from a recovered cut up magazine page with one of the wraps recovered from Dave Marsh. The links between all the callers and Styles' mobile phone were proven.

The strong links between Troy Wells and Jimmy Styles resulted in them both being charged with conspiracy to supply controlled drugs. The pair were bailed and later gave us even more evidence of their drugs supplying business.

On 27th of September 1996, I had completed my 8-hour shift at 4pm that day and was quietly sat at home when DC Hieron phoned me at 7:45pm. He had received information from a registered informant that indicated that Troy Wells had left Bristol to collect a quantity of heroin from a supplier in Swindon. He was doing the drugs run on behalf of Jimmy Styles to pay off a substantial drugs debt he had. The informant had been unable to confirm which vehicle Troy would be travelling in and I was not satisfied that we had an up-to-date car for Troy. The informant claimed that the drugs would be delivered to Styles at his home address in Warmley, where several people had gathered to get their fix. We knew of the Warmley address as Styles had moved there from Fishponds following his conspiracy charge.

Calculating the time to travel from Bristol to Swindon and back, we realised that we had little time to organise a fully staffed operation, so we had to do with a uniform officer, probationer and one other DC to assist Himey and me.

We decided that it would be too much of a risk to allow the drugs to be taken inside Styles' home so our target for this operation would be Wells. We needed to pounce on him as he arrived outside the address in Warmley and detain him for a drugs search before they changed hands. This may not provide any evidence against Styles, but his punishment would have to be the loss of the drugs purchased from Swindon.

It was too late to organise a suitable OP for the Warmley address so Himey and I found ourselves lying behind bushes on the grass about 30 metres from Styles address. We had a clear view so as soon as Wells arrived in his car, I would call a strike so our support team could pounce at the same time as we ran across the road.

There was a 50:50 chance that Wells would be arriving from our right and our support team would see him before us as they were parked discretely up the road.

It all happened so fast when at 9pm we heard a crackle on the radio, followed by silence. Suddenly a vehicle, a black Sierra turned into the street that we were watching and stopped outside the target address. The car had come from the direction that our support vehicle had been parked in, so we assumed the crackle on our radio had been them telling us.

This had to be Wells, so Himey and I ran as fast as we could across the road and into the target street.

I was shouting as I was running:

"All units strike, strike, strike".

The driver was Troy Wells and as he got out of the car, Himey grabbed hold of him before he had a chance to see us approaching. I saw Wells throw an item across the grass verge to the front garden of a nearby house. Once I established that Himey had Wells secure in handcuffs and that the passenger was so out of things on drugs that he was harmless, I ran across to retrieve what had been thrown. I called up six or seven times for the other unit to attend but there was no response.

Seven or eight people came out of the target house including Styles, they were getting a little agitated as they wanted their drugs.

One of them shouted:

"Let's get them, we can do these two".

I think the fact that Himey and I could name all the group saved us from getting a beating.

I had no torch to help with my search and no car for taking our prisoners away. I had soon located quite a large bag of pale brown powder, obviously the heroin we had been expecting. The quantity of heroin was later calculated to be just under £5000 worth. The heroin was also of a purity that indicated that it was likely to be cut with other powder before being sold to the users.

When this heroin was analysed a complicated mix of other elements was also found.

Having eventually got backup, Wells and his drugged-up accomplice were taken in custody to Staplehill police station. They were detained whilst we then went to Wells' home address to search that.

I headed the operation and the most important part of it was to ensure we entered the house as quickly as possible to prevent any evidence being disposed of. Wells' common law wife Kate had been just as disruptive as him on previous searches. The front and back doors were smashed open at the same time, and I was the first into the house. I could see Kate at the top of the stairs and on seeing me, she ran straight back into her bedroom. I shot up the stairs just in time to see Kate shove a small plastic bag into her mouth and try to swallow it. Sergeant Paul Hunt and I grabbed hold of Kate to prevent her from swallowing the drugs. We were concerned for her safety as well as not wanting to lose the evidence. We tried to force her to open her mouth by gripping her jaw and nose. It rapidly became apparent that Kate was having trouble as the plastic bag containing the heroin was stuck in her throat preventing her from breathing. I had to move quickly. I stood Kate up and walked behind her and held her in something like a bear hug. I then performed the Heimlich manoeuvre. This resulted in Kate coughing up the heroin and Paul collected our evidence. After providing further basic medical care for Kate, she was so appreciative of me saving her life that she told me where Troy's drug stash was hidden in the rear garden.

We went out into the garden and had to squeeze behind the garden shed and then reach through the fence into the neighbour's garden and recovered a half of a 'nine bar' of cannabis resin.

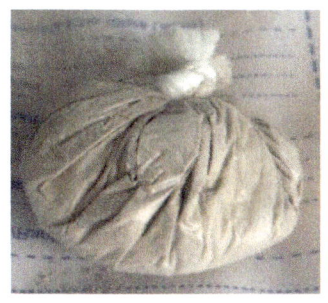

Bag of heroin from street

Bag of heroin swallowed

Piece from 9 bar cannabis

We didn't arrest Kate at this point because she was still shaken by the events earlier and she had children to look after.

It transpired that the drugs that Kate had nearly swallowed was about £150 pounds worth of heroin and when it was tested it had the identical chemical mix and strength as the bag thrown by Troy outside of Styles' house. We guessed that Troy having collected the £5000 worth of heroin from Swindon had gone home and skimmed of an amount for himself before heading to Jimmy's to hand over the remainder. Whether this was done by agreement or typical druggies ripping each other off, we will never know. No comment interviews and eventual guilty pleas at court saw Jimmy and Troy sentenced to imprisonment for both operations and their partners were given non-custodial sentences.

Chapter 4:

Hallen

We often have no idea what the neighbours are doing, and it was no difference at Hallen Industrial Estate, in Severn Road, Hallen, just 9 miles to the southeast of Bristol. The small industrial estate consisted of ten small warehouse type units that were constructed of a steel frame filled in with concrete blocks and corrugated roofs. There were all types of businesses being run from the units, two car bodywork repair shops, car repairs companies, a plant hire company, welder, carpenter, and various others.

It was the owner of one of the garages that phoned the police early on a June morning in 1999. He had over a long period of time become increasingly suspicious of three men that were using Unit H on the estate. They had been coming and going for about twelve months. When he first noticed the men, they arrived with a lot of boxed up equipment which they took inside the premises no doubt to set up their business. What made things more suspicious was that after twelve months there was no signage outside to indicate the type of business being run from the warehouse, and there were never any visits from the public. All the other warehouses had signs displayed advertising the company. The other thing that had aroused his suspicions was the fact that the men only visited their premises every two or three days. They would spend two to three hours inside and then leave. The three men kept very much to themselves, sometimes waving in acknowledgement but they never stopped to speak, unlike the other people working on the estate. The only other thing he could tell the officer was that the warehouse in question was at unit H, it had a large padlock fitted to the door and the windows were all blacked out to prevent anyone from looking inside.

The information was passed to the Force Crime Squad for further investigation. An undercover officer visited the garage owner to assess the information and to decide what or if any further action should be taken. The industrial estate was very much in the middle of the countryside with no houses overlooking the area. The officer decided that it would be too risky and too difficult to use one of the other units to carry out any observations and reported back to the office that a 'crops man' was the only option. This would mean that a specially trained covert surveillance officer in camouflage gear was needed to conceal himself in the nearby fields and bushes whilst monitoring the warehouse and photographing any callers. The garage owner was not told what action was being taken to avoid any chance of the suspicious men becoming aware.

Crops man carrying out surveillance

Within two weeks the crops man had clear photographs of all three men getting out of their car, entering the warehouse and leaving. The men did exactly as the garage owner had told the undercover officer. They arrived, entered the warehouse, stayed about two to three hours, and then left. The time of arrival varied a lot from early morning to late evening. It was always the same man driving the car, which was a blue Vauxhall Astra L21DFH. He was a white male in his 50's, slim build and had long greying wavy hair. The second male was white, 6' tall, aged in his 30's, stocky build with black hair cropped short. It was this man who always had the key to the padlock, and he would let the other two into the premises. The third man was a white male 5'9" tall slim build and with untidy long brown hair.

What they now needed was for the whole surveillance team to plot up in the vicinity of the industrial estate and to follow the men once they left in a hope of identifying who they were. It only took a week, and the Crime Squad were quite happy that they had identified all three men.

The driver was identified as Carl Bennett, he was the registered owner of the Vauxhall Astra. He lived alone in a council property in the Southville area of Bristol.

The man with the keys was identified as Paul Butler, known to the police for minor thefts and assault. He lived in a bedsit in the Totterdown area of Bristol.

The third man was identified as Butler's brother-in-law John Connolly who lived with his wife and two children in a council house in Bedminster, Bristol.

The Crime Squad had successfully followed Bennett as he dropped off the other two at their homes, so it took little effort to confirm their identities and to know where they lived. Police previous arrest photographs of the targets were used to verify the names.

On Wednesday the 1st of September 1999, the Crime Squad followed the men to Kings Developments Ltd in the Bishopston area of Bristol, where Paul Butler and John Connolly spent twenty minutes inside before returning to the car and heading out to Hallen. When enquiries were made into the development company, it appeared to be a business that rented out commercial premises to people.

On Friday the 1st of October, Paul Butler and John Connolly paid another short visit to

Kings Developments, and shortly after the men drove off, a member of the surveillance team decamped from his vehicle and made enquiries with the manager of Kings. The manager explained that the two men had come in to pay their monthly rent as they did on the 1st of every month. The rent was for a warehouse at Unit H, Hallen Industrial Park. The men were very good customers and always paid on time and in cash. The manager had no idea what they were using the warehouse for, he supplied a name for the dark-haired man as David Smith.

The next thing the Crime Squad wanted to know was what was inside the warehouse. They had their own procedures and authorities to allow them to enter premises covertly. They had specially trained officers who could pick locks so arranged that the following night, under the cover of darkness, they would take a quick look inside Unit H. There were two padlocks to pick in fact, the outer door, and an inner door. These proved no problem, and it was immediately obvious what the unit was being used for. There was a large cannabis growing facility filling the main area. Not wanting to remain on the premises for any longer than necessary, the officer left and replaced the padlocks.

It was now time to pass over the investigation to the district CID at Staplehill and that was where I was introduced to the case. I attended a private meeting where the Crime Squad supervisor briefed me on the investigation. There had been lots of information gathered but nothing had been put into evidential format.

Various ideas were thrown about but, in the end, we planned to have a day of warrants. It was felt that we could already place the three suspects at the premises on several occasions so there was no need to catch them inside. Cannabis factories are well known for being dangerous places due to the high levels of electricity about and vast quantities of water. It was safer to search the premises with no suspects present to avoid the possibility of a fight breaking out in the dangerous environment. We had four warrants sworn out, one for Unit H and the other three were the suspects' home addresses. We accepted that there was a chance that the suspects would not be located straight away but with all the addresses searched, any evidence would be secured. We knew that suspects not arrested would quickly become aware of our interest in them and may go into hiding.

I got together a large team of district detectives and district crime unit officers from both Staplehill and Broadbury Road police areas. We all met on the morning of Friday the 5th of November for me to brief everyone. Detective Constable Andy Hailes and I were going to take the lead on the case, conduct the interviews and prepare any court papers. We would lead the search warrant at Unit H and once the search was underway, we would go immediately to Butler's bedsit in Totterdown.

Broadbury Road District Crime Unit were to deal with the warrants at Bedminster and Southville. The warrants at unit H and Connolly's Bedminster address were to be executed simultaneously at 11:45am. The shortage of resources prevented us from searching all four properties at the same time.

At precisely 11:45am, a set of giant bolt croppers were used to remove the outer padlock at Unit H. When we pulled open the outer door, we were given access to a small area about 3m x 4m in size. This room contained an old desk, chair, and a waste bin. There were piles of clear plastic gloves, white paper suits and paper over shoes. It looked like this was the changing room before you enter the main warehouse. In the bin were some old used gloves and shoe covers as well as a crumpled-up receipt for the purchase of sandwiches and drinks three days earlier. There was a strong smell of cannabis even in this section of the building. I had become accustomed to that smell over many years of seizing cannabis. The pungent smell of cannabis will quickly give you a headache so this could account for the suspects spending no more than a couple hours at a time in the building.

The bolt croppers were out again to cut off the inner padlock. We were then faced with a large black plastic sheet draped down in front of us. Before we went any further you could feel the heat coming from within. We pushed past this plastic screen and were faced with a mass of 2m tall cannabis plants, they were all very green and very healthy-looking plants. The room was extremely well lit up providing all the light the plants needed to grow. There was no-one on the premises, so we took our time to take in what we had.

The main room was divided into two sections, the fully grown flowering plants were in the front half but it looked like about a third of them had recently been harvested. The back section had equally healthy plants but only about 1m tall and not flowering. The system they were using to grow the plants was a hydroponic system, supported by powerful lighting and heating. There was a cupboard full of chemicals and gadgets.

I had made a point after having taken over the case from the Force Crime Squad of getting to know a little more about hydroponic growing of cannabis plants. So just in case you may also be interested to know, I will explain a little about it to you.

As the name suggests, hydroponics is a soilless method of growing plants, in this case, cannabis using water. Cannabis plants are grown in trays, buckets or baskets filled with a growing medium such as rockwool, and the plants are suspended over a tank full of water. The water is filled with all the nutrients the plants need to survive and thrive and air stones are used to aerate the tank.

Hydroponic plants grow much faster than those in soil, usually 30–50% faster and often provide larger yields. The main reason for this is that nutrient levels are regularly checked.

With a hydroponic system, nutrients are more easily absorbed by plants grown in water rather than soil as the nutrients enter directly into the plants roots.

The growers also tend to make regular checks of the pH of the water to ensure an optimal growing environment. A pH of 5.5–5.8 is preferred during general growing, and a pH of 6 during flowering. My research suggested to me that we could expect to find a pH testing kit as the growers use these to take regular readings and adjust the pH when necessary.

Hydroponic cannabis has an ideal temperature of 20°C. Temperatures are often monitored using a thermometer in conjunction with water heaters. The heater being adjusted if the temperatures are too low.

Before we started our search, a Scenes of Crime officer took a series of photographs for use in court. We disconnected the electric supply and called out an electrician from the electricity board to make sure it was safe. The meter for the electric supply was in a box outside the premises so the meters could be read without entering. We photographed and took a meter reading.

From the premises, we seized the following items: powerful lighting and light hangers, water heaters, water thermometers, fans, ventilation tubing to circulate the heat, growing trays, pumps, rockwool, pH testers and an assortment of nutrients.

We had in the region of a hundred plants which we counted and from some, we removed sample leaves that we would send to forensic scientists for them to test the strength of the cannabis and to estimate the street value. The scientists having carried out their testing and having viewed the photographs gave us a street value of around 40K.

So, what happened at the other warrants. John Connolly was not at home; his wife was present when the house was searched. An assortment of documentation was seized relating to his phone, a car, an album of photographs which included photographs of his brother-in-law Paul Butler. An address book containing Butler's and Bennett's home addresses was seized showing an association with the others.

DC Hailes and I searched Butler's address in Totterdown, we were allowed into the communal hallway by another resident. On the hall shelf were several items of post addressed to Mr P Butler and one addressed to Mr J Connolly. It was necessary for us to force our entry to the upstairs bedsit and in doing so we split the door frame. It was clear once inside that we had the right address but the only things of interest that we seized were four items of clothing that were very distinctive and matched clothing in the Force Crime Squad surveillance images outside of the Hallen warehouse.

The team that searched for Bennett found him at home and his Vauxhall Astra was parked outside. A small quantity of personal cannabis bush was lying on the coffee table when they entered the lounge. A search of the flat resulted in the seizure of his phone, items of clothing including a white paper suit splashed in paint and an address book. Carl was arrested and made no comment. He, in fact, made no comment to every question that Andy and I put to him in interview. He was made aware of all the evidence proving that he was linked to the address in Hallen but he remained silent. He declined to admit even knowing Paul Butler or John Connolly. Carl was bailed to return to the police station in order that the recovered plants could be tested, the other two suspects be arrested, and statements obtained from those people able to supply evidence for court. Before leaving, Bennett requested the return of his car and keys that we had seized. He was given his blue Vauxhall Astra L21DFH back not knowing that his car had also given up the fingerprints of Connolly and Butler.

We continued our enquiries to try and locate and arrest Butler and Connolly but this was proving a lot harder that we had hoped. They were deliberately trying to avoid us. We also had our other CID enquiries to deal with, I got involved in the investigations of two murders, several deceptions, and burglaries as well as court appearances during the following months. The only reason I tell you this is, so you understand why things took so long.

We could however fit in the gathering of evidence for this investigation amongst our other work. When booking in all the hydroponics equipment at Staplehill police station we had noticed that several of the items contained the same suppliers label indicating that they had been purchased from a specialist supplier in Bristol on the outskirts of Hartcliffe. I should point out that hydroponics growing can quite legally be used to grow most type of plants, it is only the cultivation of cannabis that is controlled. We obtained a statement from the company that sold the equipment although they could not give details of who had purchased the items. They were able to tell us that the items were purchased 18 months earlier and were paid for in cash. The customer gave the name of David Smith. What was important to us was the knowledge that the equipment had cost £2,000 to purchase.

The receipt that we had found in the waste bin in the front section of Unit H was for three packs of sandwiches, a bottle of water and two cans of coke. It was a McColls receipt dated the 2nd of November 1999 and timed 5.36pm, only three days before we raided the property. The McColls was located only two miles away in Lawrence Weston. From the CCTV at McColls, we were easily able to identify Butler and Connolly buying the food. We seized the video tape and obtained a statement from the manager.

The paper suit splashed in paint recovered from Carl Bennett's home was the same brand as those found in the Hallen warehouse. It was likely he had decided to take one from the warehouse to use for painting at home.

On the 16th of November 1999, Andy Hailes and I attended at Kings Developments Ltd in Bishopston where we spoke with the leasing manager. He made a statement that on Thursday the 2nd of April 1998, three men called at their premises interested in renting the warehouse at Unit H, Hallen. They had already viewed the building from the outside by themselves and were satisfied that the location and building were suitable for their business. The men never discussed their intended use of the building and agreed to the rental fees and paid cash to cover the first three months. It was also agreed that they would pay for the electricity supply which Kings staff would read quarterly from the meter located outside the building. The manager supplied us with the original Tenancy agreement and the electricity reading sheet showing the regular high usage of electricity. He explained that he had spoken almost exclusively to the tallest male who had cropped black hair and it was him who gave the name David Smith. (Paul Butler, we assumed). He described all three men but said it was always the same man who paid in cash monthly by visiting the Kings' office. David Smith suggested that they wanted the premises for at least two years, but it could well be extended later.

Andy and I then drove up to Hallen Industrial Estate to speak with Mr Harris who was the garage owner who had first contacted the police about his suspicions back in June. Having spoken to a Crime Squad officer, Mr Harris wondered if anything was being done about his information. He had decided to keep records of anything unusual involving the men at Unit H. I took a statement from Mr Harris and included in it two occasions of specific interest.

He had recorded that on the 3rd of October at 11:15am, instead of all three men arriving in the blue Vauxhall Astra L21DFH as was normal, only the one man arrived. He was the man that always drove that car (Carl Bennett the vehicle owner from description). This man parked up and waited outside the warehouse and was sat there for 18 minutes when a second car arrived. This was a red Renault R567CLR. This car contained the other two men, the passenger being the tallest man with black hair (Paul Butler) and the driver was slim build with long brown straggly hair (John Connolly). As they got out and spoke with each other Mr Harris was sure that the driver of the Astra referred to the other driver as John. The passenger, the tallest man opened the door by the padlock. All three entered but only remained there for about ten minutes. The driver of the Astra and the passenger of the Renault left Unit H and padlocked the other driver inside the warehouse. The Astra driver got in his vehicle with the other man as the front seat passenger and they drove off. It was not until 1:35pm that the two men returned and let the third out of the premises.

The other incident that Mr Harris had recorded was at 6:15pm on the 2nd of November all three men arrived in the blue Astra. They entered Unit H and were carrying what looked like piles of empty bin liners. Mr Harris could not say when they left as he finished work at about 6:30pm.

There were many arrest attempts for both Paul Butler and John Connolly, we searched their home addresses several times as well as the addresses of their families. I believed that it was possible that John had moved in with his mother in a block of flats in Bedminster as on three separate occasions I had sighted the red Renault R567CLR parked outside.

On the 20th of April, we had still not located John or Paul despite our best efforts. At 10:45am, I was parked in the vicinity of John's mother's house when I sighted the red Renault R567CLR driving along St Johns Lane, Bedminster. I followed the vehicle whilst calling for assistance to stop the car. The vehicle driver had obviously realised that he was being followed and started to drive erratically and fast. The car swerved left into Torpoint Road and I followed. As I turned the corner, I could see the Renault was abandoned and empty in the middle of the road. The driver was running off towards Lynton Road and I recognised him as John Connolly. Unfortunately, he was soon lost to sight and an extensive search of the area failed to locate him.

Paul Butler was being equally as evasive. Failing to show up to collect his benefits on three occasions but we never gave up.

On the 15th of May 2000 our luck changed. I had tasked the Broadbury Road District Crime Unit to target John Connolly, supplying them with all the information I had. At 8:45am, as I started work, the DCU supervisor phoned to tell me that John Connolly was in custody at Trinity Road police station. Andy Hailes and I conducted several interviews with him, and he surprisingly decided to give an account for his links to Unit H at Hallen Industrial Estate. I guess that he had plenty of time whilst evading our capture to come up with a story. He refused to name either of the other two men he had visited the premises at Hallen with but claimed that he had only ever entered through the first padlocked door and had never been any further inside. He would not make any comment when I pointed out to him how strong the smell of cannabis was, even in the front area of the warehouse. He would also not account for spending over two hours on the 3rd of October 1999 locked inside the 3m x 4m section of the building. He claimed to have no knowledge what the unit was being used for and did not accept that he was concerned in the cultivation of cannabis. We had sufficient evidence to charge Connolly with cultivation and he was detained for court. He later appeared jointly with Carl Bennett.

Eventually it was Paul Butler's turn to get arrested. We had learnt that he frequently visited the local Dillons store in Totterdown, and on the third time of parking up and waiting for his appearance, he eventually turned up. It was 12:05pm on Monday the 19th of June and as soon as Paul left Dillons, Andy and I were up alongside him, detaining him. We took him to our police car and told him he was being arrested for the production of controlled drugs and possession of drugs with intent to supply, he was told it was in connection with an industrial estate in Hallen. After cautioning him he replied:

" Yes, what took you so long".

He was taken to Staplehill police station for interview. Paul went no comment during interview and was charged with the offences and detained for court.

When each of the offenders were charged, they were photographed, fingerprinted, and had their DNA taken as was standard procedure. Their fingerprints came in very useful as we had several matches with prints found during our investigation.

Paul Butler's fingerprints, as well as being in Carl Bennett's Astra, were found on the tenancy agreement seized from the manager of Kings Developments Ltd. John Connolly's fingerprints were found in the Astra and on the McColls receipt recovered from the waste bin in the front section of Unit H. He had also been careless enough to leave his prints on the cupboard containing nutrients within the main warehouse growing area. Carl Bennett's fingerprints were found on two pieces of growing apparatus from the main warehouse. The cases against all three was getting stronger.

Four weeks later, I received a report of five DNA matches between Paul Butler's DNA and five burglaries. The burglaries were all in new houses under construction. The houses were nearly complete but not occupied. The offender on each occasion had forced entry through a rear door and had dismantled and stolen the central heating boilers. Paul Butler was quite clumsy as he cut himself each time and left his DNA in the form of blood on the boiler pipework left behind. The burglaries were in two separate construction sites, three houses in Stoke Bishop that were burgled in February 1998 and two houses on a construction site in Bromsgrove burgled in January 1998.

Paul Butler was arrested by us for the burglaries and as you might expect refused to answer any of the questions we put to him. He was charged with five separate burglary offences.

All three would normally have appeared at court together to face the joint charges but Paul Butler failed to appear for court so a warrant for his arrest was issued.

Bennett and Connolly pleaded guilty to the cultivation of cannabis and possessing drugs with intent to supply. Bennett was sentenced to 12 months imprisonment and Connelly 18 months. The harvested crop of cannabis was never recovered so they no doubt made quite a profit from the business. Paul Butler was eventually arrested for the fail to appear warrant. He pleaded guilty to the drugs offences and to five burglaries. He was sentenced to 2 years imprisonment.

Sex

Chapter 1:

Kerb Crawlers

Having been a Detective Constable for the past 6 years at Bishopsworth Police station, my career took a significant change of direction when in 1989, I was promoted to the position of uniform sergeant based at Trinity Road police station. The Trinity district included Lawrence Hill, Easton, St Phillips, Redfield, Whitehall, Barton Hill, St Jude's, St Paul's, Eastville and Redcliffe.

On my first day on the district, I was told that I was to become the St Paul's beat supervisor responsible for 5 constables. My role was to work every shift with my team, patrolling the St Paul's area, leaving the remaining supervisor to cover the rest of the district.

St Paul's was a typical inner urban area with a large multi-ethnic population. It was a lively neighbourhood, right in the heart of the city centre, but was one of the most deprived parts of Bristol. The main policing problems were drugs, street prostitution and anti-social behaviour.

Only 9 years earlier in April 1980, the police had carried out a raid on the Afro-Caribbean owned Black and White Café in Grosvenor Road, St Pauls. The officers began trying to remove the confiscated alcohol from the premises when they came under attack from mainly black youths who pelted them with bottles and bricks, causing the police officers to vacate the area. I was involved on the very tail end of the riots when I was part of a large team of officers who supported the district and attempted to bring calm back to the area.

The Bristol riots also sparked disorder in other parts of the country such as Brixham. Racism was blamed as the catalyst for the riots. Fortunately, by 1989, things had calmed down greatly in St Pauls, but drugs and prostitution were still a major problem.

I spent my first three weeks attached to acting sergeant Malcolm Cobb, he was an experienced officer who knew the St Pauls beat well. He was waiting to get promoted so was temporary sergeant covering the St Pauls beat. I was going to be taking over his duties, but I needed to get as much knowledge from him about policing in this type of area. Malcolm showed me the main illicit drinking houses, the drug dealers, their drug dens, and he also pointed out the key areas where the street prostitutes plied their trade. He was able to introduce me to many prostitutes who would speak openly about why they chose that line of business. It was fascinating to see how stringently the girls kept to their own special street corner or house doorway. They also had set locations that they would direct their punters to take them for sex. Most of the girls had pimps who 'looked after them' but who also took advantage of them.

My team and I became very efficient at arresting the prostitutes. The Street Offences Act of 1959 detailed two main offences.

'It shall be an offence for a common prostitute to **loiter** or **solicit** in a street or public place for the purpose of prostitution.'

Malcolm taught me that the offence of soliciting was the much easier to prove. You required the presence of both the prostitute and the punter negotiating the sexual services of the prostitute. You would wait for the punter to approach the prostitute and for them to walk off or drive off together before you made the arrest. The fact that the female was a common prostitute, with previous convictions and the male was not an associate would normally be enough to get an admission and eventually a successful prosecution.

Loitering required a person to persistently hang around in a street or public place for the purpose of prostitution. It was therefore necessary to prove what the prostitute intended by loitering on the street corner and to maintain a record to show persistence.

I soon became as good as the rest of my team. I could arrest a prostitute for soliciting, process her at Trinity Road police station, charge her and release her, all within the hour. What that meant was that she was likely out on the street corner again earning money to pay off the fine she would get at court.

It was not uncommon for prostitutes when being sentenced to have 50+ charges against them and to receive a fine of £2 per offence. There were lots of discussions about the benefits of making prostitution legal, where sex would take place indoors, in a safe environment and with regular medical checks to reduce the risk of sexually transmitted diseases. It would also reduce the numbers of pimps that normally took 70% of the girl's earnings in exchange for protection. The pimps did serve a purpose as they would record the registration numbers of cars that the girls got into. This was useful in cases where they had not returned within an hour or if the girls were beaten up or robbed. The pimps, through the prostitute, would be able to supply us with the offenders' car details and the offenders would be quickly arrested. The girls were also very good at getting the word out to other prostitutes of vehicles and punters to avoid due to their violent nature or unacceptable sexual preferences.

I recall on one of my early days with Malcolm Cobb, he pointed out to me a kerb crawler, I looked across and the car he spoke about looked like any other car so I asked Malcolm how he knew it was a kerb crawler. He explained that they were nearly always quite new cars with one male occupant. They would drive around slowing down at various locations where prostitutes loitered on the street corners. The most significant thing was that they would drive round a specific circuit taking in all the prostitute haunts and could be seen circulating every ten minutes. It had been the third time he had seen that specific car in the last 20 minutes touring the recognised kerb crawler circuit.

The term kerb crawler is defined as someone who will simply drive slowly along the edge of the road in search of a prostitute.

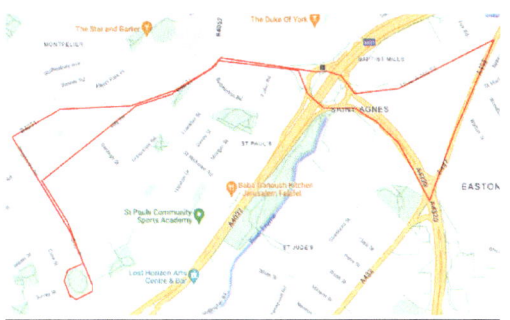

Kerb Crawlers circuit around St Pauls in 1989

I had only been working at Trinity Road for about three months when I was asked to run an anti-Kerb crawling patrol operation. The numbers of prostitutes standing in the street soliciting for clients had been steadily increasing and the number of kerb crawlers looking for sex had too. We wanted to concentrate on reducing the kerb crawlers this time rather than just arrest more and more prostitutes. The plan was to monitor the activities of kerb crawlers and to stop them immediately after they approached and spoke with a prostitute or picked them up in their car. The prostitute would be sent packing and the kerb crawler would be spoken to and given a written and verbal warning. Their names, addresses and vehicle details would be taken, and they would be handed a prepared letter that explained, if they were caught again kerb crawling, a second and final warning would be sent by post to their home address.

The final warning letter pointed out that under the Sexual Offences Act 1985, the kerb crawler commits an offence if he persistently solicits a woman for the purpose of prostitution or if his behaviour caused annoyance or nuisance to others. The maximum fine for kerb crawling in 1989 was £400.

The worry to the kerb crawler was the fact that the letter risked falling into the hands of other people living at the same address, such as a wife or partner. The anti-kerb crawling operation seemed to do the trick and kerb crawling numbers reduced drastically. The men did not wish to attend court, risk their partners finding out or to pay a fine.

The government many years later understood the annoyance caused by kerb crawlers and brought in the 2003 Sexual Offences Act which increased the maximum fine to £1000 and made proving the offence much easier by removing the need to show persistence.

It was whilst on one of the kerb crawling patrols that I had a more intimate dealing with one prostitute. It was normal to see 10 – 15 prostitutes hanging around on street corners. They were friendly enough but got to know me as someone who would regularly arrest them, deal with them fairly and then leave them alone for the rest of that night. We accepted each other's role in the area.

Although it was normal to work in twos, for some reason on this evening I was alone. It was 2am and a cold wet morning, so the prostitute numbers were down slightly. I was driving very slowly along City Road towards the city centre. I could see a short distance ahead of me a young lady walking unsteadily in the middle of the road and my first thought was that she was drunk and may need assistance. I slowed up as I approached, she looked up. She then lifted her skirt and because she had no knickers on, she exposed everything to me.

I stopped the car and wound my window down only to recognise her as one of the local prostitutes. I will refer to her as Bernice rather than name and shame her. Bernice came over and said:

"*Did you see anything you would like?*"

Being professional and very polite I said:

"*No thank you*".

She continued by saying:

"Go on, I've had a PC and an Inspector, but I've never had a Sergeant before".

I pointed out that she wasn't going to have this sergeant and that if she didn't get on home, she would be seeing another sergeant namely the Custody Sergeant. Bernice walked off cussing and no doubt went home because I didn't see her again that night.

She did apologise to me many days later when I was driving around with a colleague in the car but did it in such a way that I'm sure my colleague wondered what had occurred between the two of us when she suggested that I may wish to see her naked again!

The street prostitutes were normally quite a chatty friendly group of ladies, but you could tell how street wise they had become after years of doing tricks. They normally insisted on the use of condoms and if the punter refused then no sexual contact took place. Some of course just didn't care and if they could be paid more without condoms being used, they would agree. They tended to choose that lifestyle due to the need to feed a drugs habit or to get money to put food on the table. With so much of their money being taken by their pimps they were rarely well off and lived from day to day. I recall one prostitute was still taking punters when she was 5 months pregnant as she had two other children to feed. The prostitutes had their regular clients that they were very friendly with. They knew they could rely on their regulars to seek them out once a week and provide that regular income.

Chapter 2:

Brothel

A brothel is a place where people engage in sexual activity with prostitutes. These can often be disguised as massage parlours offering a wide range of sexual services and having nothing to do with holistic style massages.

Any premises, such as private flats, saunas, massage parlours, may be classified as a brothel if they are used by more than one man or woman for the purpose of prostitution.

Most people want the prostitutes off the streets, so brothels were considered a way of achieving this. It was understood that prostitution would never be eliminated but if it were to take place within brothels, then the women would be in a safer environment and less likely to be attacked. The sexual acts would not be taking place in a dark quiet location with only the prostitute and punter present but instead in the comfort of a warm indoor environment, with other prostitutes in the building.

It was normally the location of the brothel that brought it to the notice of the police. A premises away from residential areas rarely caused any issues and the brothel was left to its own devices. Occasionally brothels were opened up in residential houses and these would quickly cause a nuisance to local residents and complaints to the police would come in thick and fast.

The next case was one of these residential brothels that attracted many complaints from the residents. The general tone of the complaints was, that the house was only occupied during the day and left empty overnight. Every morning at about 10am three or four ladies would arrive at the house. By 11am a slow stream of lone male callers would enter the address, stay for 40-50 minutes, and then leave. The ladies closed shop at about midnight. The complainants did not want their children exposed to this activity and several of the neighbours had been approached by men seeking the address. It was clear to everyone what was happening at the house, and it was lowering the neighbourhood.

On the Staplehill district, most nuisance type complaints were discussed at a weekly priorities meeting to decide which matters should be investigated further and by whom. The District Detective Inspector or Detective Sergeants would attend these meetings to explain the CID caseload and to take on new investigations if the district required it. It was my turn to attend the priorities meeting on Monday 13th December 1999 and it was here that an illegal brothel being run from a residential address in Soundwell Road was discussed.

I agreed that I would take on the investigation with Detective Constable Ian Hieron from the CID as long as support would be available from the District Crime Unit who were trained in surveillance. The initial plan was for me to pay the premises a visit overtly, to speak with the occupants and let them know about the complaints. They would be asked to vacate the premises and find somewhere more suitable away from houses. This approach had been successful in the past but if the ladies or their boss declined to heed my request, we would take the matter further.

I visited the premises on Thursday 16th December at 1pm. There were three women present in the house when I arrived. I immediately introduced myself and told them about the complaints that we had received. I was shown around the house by Celia Black who appeared to be the more senior of the girls aged 23years. She was white, 5'6" tall, slim build, with shoulder length wavy blond hair. She was dressed in an open necked white blouse, dark blue mini skirt, and long white boots. I recorded her name, address, and phone number for my records.

The house was in Soundwell Road a short distance from the junction with Page Road, Bristol. It was a two bedroomed terrace house with two reception rooms and a kitchen. The room on the right as you entered the front door was previously used as a lounge, but it was now laid out as a reception room, with a table and five office style chairs. The room to the left of the front door which had previously been a dining room had a double bed in the centre of the back wall. The bed was made and alongside it was a dressing table with a lamp and radio on it. Also on top of the dressing table was a box containing numerous unopened packets of condoms. There were two bottles of massage cream, three boxes of tissues and a large candle. There was nothing else in the room except an empty waste bin on the other side of the bed. The curtains were drawn making the room very dark and dingy. I was shown the two bedrooms located upstairs and these were laid out identically to the bedroom downstairs. None of the rooms had any of the standard massage tables used by professional masseurs. There were no wardrobes or other indication that the house was lived in.

The kitchen showed very little sign that the house was lived in either. There was a kettle and a fridge but no cooker or other electrical appliances.

I took the names, addresses and phone numbers of the other two ladies in the house. Debbie Jones aged 19 years. She was 5'4" tall, slim build with long straight dark hair that was halfway down her back. She was wearing a short black dress, zipped down the front but opened to expose a red and black lacy bra. She wore red high heeled shoes. Louise Brown aged 20 years 5'7" tall slim build with shoulder length bleached blond hair. She wore a short white lacy dress which was partially see thorough and showing her black bra and knickers underneath. She had on black high heeled shoes.

I explained to all the ladies that it was quite clear what was occurring at the premises and that it was an offence for a person to keep, to manage, or assist in the management of, a brothel to which people resort for practices involving prostitution. I told them that if they continued to work on the premises, I would gather evidence to prosecute them for running a brothel. I suggested that they move elsewhere that did not attract complaints from the public. They listened to what I had to say and at no time did they deny what I was suggesting. I left saying that I would check if they had gone within the next month.

On 7th February 2000 we commenced observations on the address in Soundwell Road to confirm for ourselves that the premises was still being used as a brothel and not a place of residence. Within the week we had confirmed our belief. Every morning at about 10am a Black BMW motor car index S300ATG would pull up outside the house, the three girls Celia, Debbie, and Louise dressed casually in jeans and tee shirts would vacate the vehicle all carrying holdalls and go into the premises. The driver rarely went inside but drove off towards Kingswood. He would sometimes return with two other ladies who at that stage we had not identified.

The car owner we were able to identify as Anthony Thomas Gough, 29 years old, who was known to the police for violence and drugs offences.

All the indications were that Gough was using the girls as prostitutes and he was the person behind the running of the brothel. We made enquiries into the owners of the Soundwell Road address and found that it was on a short-term rental. It had been rented out by Anthony Gough for an initial period of six months. He had paid cash for his deposit but had supplied his home address details and a mobile number of 0799xxxx123.

I had decided with my team that our focus would be on safeguarding the women as often within brothels the women are coerced into working. We would seek to offer them assistance from health professionals or social workers and maybe persuade them to get out of the sex business altogether. We would hope that they could be persuaded to provide evidence against the person managing the brothel, who we believed to be Anthony Gough.

To get the girls on our side we first wanted to gather the evidence that sexual services were being offered for payment on the premises. We decided against sending in undercover police officers to pose as customers even though I had several volunteers. I decided a better approach would be to observe the premises and to follow the punters from the address and to question them afterwards about their visit to the house. This we started on 10th February and continued for 5 days, stopping only two customers a day to reduce the chance of our activity getting back to the girls.

When the men were approached and told that we wished to discuss their visit to a brothel in Soundwell Road, the majority were initially shocked and very nervous. They were reassured when we explained that we were not interested in charging them with any offence but were keen to gain evidence against whoever was running the brothel. Six of the men were persuaded to make written statements about exactly what had occurred in the house, albeit they were reluctant to go into detail about the sexual acts they had paid for. They had been offered a range of sexual acts by the girls, such as full sex, anal sex, oral sex, and masturbation. All were told that a condom had to be used and would be provided by the girl. Some of the men had been given a choice of which of the three girls they wished, and on one occasion the customer admitted paying for two girls at the same time. One of the men could also recall that another bedroom was in use at the same time he was there. Most of the men had learnt about the address as it was being advertised as a massage parlour in the Bristol Evening Post newspaper. The advert included a mobile phone number 0799xxxx678 and a post code BS16. Having seen the advert, the men phoned the number and spoke to a girl called Rachel. It was clear to them that more than a massage was on offer, and they were invited around to the address to discuss prices and details of what precise service they wanted to pay for. It was only at that point that they were told the address.

I don't have the exact advert available, but it read something like this:

'New luxurious massage parlour opened up BS16. We have several girls for you to choose from, all are keen to please and meet your needs. Just explain how we can help, and you can be sure to leave totally satisfied. Phone Rachel on 0799xxxx678 to discuss prices and arrange a visit.'

The background of the men was varied, the age range we came across was 24 to 60 years old, most were married men and employed. There were labourers and professionals. One man I specifically recall was an anaesthetist at one of the local hospitals. He made a statement on the Monday evening but by the Thursday morning he called at the station to explain that he had been so worried he had been unable to sleep, and it was affecting his judgement at work. He seemed happier once I was able to explain that our plan was to arrest the girls with plenty of evidence in a hope that they would become witnesses against the brothel manager. If the girls cooperated, then all the statements from the callers like him would be unused evidence.

When we made enquiries with the Bristol Evening Post, we found that a Mr Anthony Gough using phone number 0799xxxx123 had placed many other similar adverts during the previous two years but quoting different post codes including BS7 and BS23. Each advert stated "Phone Rachel", but different mobile numbers were then used. There were no specific addresses for us to check but one of the post codes BS23 indicated an area in Weston-Super-Mare.

It was now time to question the girls. They had failed to heed my warnings so we would now be paying them a visit to call a halt to their activities. We chose a Wednesday to raid the address in Soundwell Road as this had previously been a busy day for them. The surveillance team told us that a new client had just arrived at the premises and a few minutes after that, one of our male undercover officers phoned 0799xxxx678, asking for Rachel. It was agreed he could go straight round to the house and the woman gave him the full address, which luckily was the house we were watching. As the front door was opened to the undercover officer, five other search officers entered the property at the same time. The male client came out of one of the upstairs bedrooms, looking quite sheepish. He was taken to one side, and his details were obtained, and he was given advice about using such premises before being allowed to leave.

The house was searched and numerous exhibits seized that supported the evidence gathered to date that the house was being used as a brothel. Six used condoms were found in waste bins, these were photographed before being destroyed. The girl's holdalls were found, and they contained their jeans and t-shirts and day clothes. All three were dressed in their working clothes which were much more revealing.

Celia, Debbie and Louise were the only prostitutes present and they were invited back to Staplehill police station for questioning. They were not arrested but agreed to help on the understanding that if we arrested the man behind the business, he would be given bail conditions not to contact them. Ian Hieron and I spoke jointly with the girls first and explained our investigation to date. Celia confirmed that Anthony Gough paid the rental for the house and paid for advertisements to be placed in the Bristol Evening Post and The Sunday Sport newspaper. Mr Gough would collect the girls from their home addresses each morning and take them to the house. It was when he took them home in the evening that he would take his substantial cut of the money. The girls ended up with about £20 per client only. Celia stated that she was given a mobile phone by Mr Gough to be used only for taking calls from clients. She was to answer to the name of Rachel, and she handed us the phone 0799xxxx678. We asked them about the other two girls we had seen Mr Gough with at the address on previous dates and they gave us the names of Samantha, and Vanessa who normally worked at a separate house in Weston-Super-Mare. Celia and Debbie had both worked at the Weston address themselves on a couple of occasions and were willing to point it out to us if necessary.

Celia also mentioned two previous addresses in Filton Avenue where she and four other prostitutes had worked for Anthony Gough, but they had been closed on Mr Gough's instructions. The details of the four prostitutes were supplied to us. Himey and I traced them and although they spoke with us, they declined to make statements through fear of retribution.

Himey took a statement from Celia and Louise, and I took a statement from Debbie. The girls were all given information as to where they could get support to get out of prostitution and support for protecting themselves against sexually transmitted diseases. The Soundwell Road premises were closed immediately and the girls were not seen there again.

Celia's involvement in the brothel was considered as falling short of being a 'Madame' (Organiser and controller of the brothel). She was certainly responsible for the day to day running of affairs when Anthony Gough was not about, and she may have recruited some of the prostitutes, but she was clearly not the owner and had little control of the financial affairs. None of the girls were charged with any offences.

It was only one week later when I learnt that Debbie had in fact given us a false name. Her real name being Debbie Johnson and she was only 16 years old, soon to be seventeen. She had left home 6 months earlier, following arguments with her parents and was living with Celia. This caused a slight issue because being only 16 years old, she should have been questioned and statement taken in the presence of an appropriate adult. I arranged to meet up with her again and she agreed to be seen with a social worker acting as an appropriate adult to retake her statement. The social worker would also act as a longer-term contact for her.

Himey and I found ourselves travelling up to the headquarters of the Sunday Sports newspaper to speak with their classified advertisements manager. He had located a large number of ads placed in their newspaper going back two years. The ads were placed using the name Anthony Gough or the phone number 0799xxxx123. The ads were all of a similar nature to those in the Bristol Evening Post and advertising 'Massage parlours' with a choice of girls. The mobile number varied but the contact's name of Rachel remained consistent. The post code for the earlier premises was given as GL52, which was Cheltenham, Gloucestershire.

We spoke again with Celia; she could not supply any details of addresses in Cheltenham but was aware that Anthony Gough used to run houses there. Celia had managed to get hold of Samantha and Vanessa from the Weston-Super-Mare brothel and both had agreed to meet us. Celia mentioned that she had received verbal threats from Anthony Gough since the brothel had been closed. He was aware that he was under investigation and threatened to harm anyone who made a statement against him. We spoke about her having a police alarm fitted at her home address, but she declined the offer. She was told that he would be arrested soon.

It was through Samantha that we learnt that the property they had used in Weston was a residential house in Walliscote Road, it was semi-detached and with three bedrooms allowing four girls to work there regularly. Samantha had been given a mobile phone by Anthony Gough to use for business only and she was told to use the name Rachel whenever she took calls. She had to hand over most of the daily takings to Mr Gough when he visited her during the afternoons. Anthony Gough had a friend to pick up and drop off Samantha and the other girls each day. Samantha and Vanessa had spoken to the other girls that worked at the Weston property, but they did not want to speak with the police. Samantha agreed to wind up business at Walliscote Road and if Mr Gough asked why, she would tell him that the police had called and warned them off.

We contacted DC Tim Holt from the force Financial Investigations Unit, and he agreed to investigate the financial affairs of Anthony Gough for any evidence that could progress our investigation. Tim proved very useful to us and other than showing the amount of money Anthony Gough was making, Tim was also able to give us details of two houses in Cheltenham that Mr Gough paid rent on up until 18 months ago. The houses were in Evesham Road and Clarence Road, both GL52.

The police in Gloucester were able to tell us that they had been aware of brothels being run from the addresses and that they had closed soon after they were given a warning of potential prosecution. The Gloucester police only had one name connected to the brothel. We traced Vicky Hill who told us that she had worked as a receptionist only at the Evesham Road brothel, she knew what the address was being used for. She had only been working there for two weeks to help and earn a little cash, when the police visited and warned them to close it down. She saw Anthony Gough at the premises twice during that time. She declined to make a statement to us. The current occupants of the addresses were aware that the house had previously been used as a brothel, but they had no details of anyone involved. One of the owners mentioned that for weeks after he moved in, he would get male callers looking for a massage parlour.

Having Anthony Gough's phone number and the numbers of all the girls, we were soon able to show the frequency of contact between them. Anthony Gough would phone Samantha and Celia two or three times daily and very infrequently call the others. It appeared Samantha was the day-to-day organiser of things in Walliscote Road.

We had by now spoken to fifteen prostitutes that had been used in various Brothels run by Anthony Gough, taken statements from five and gathered evidence from the advertising in newspapers and the rental of properties, so were ready to question Mr Gough.

At 10am on Tuesday 4th July 2000 Anthony Gough attended along with his legal advisor, at Staplehill police station by appointment. He was arrested for the management of several brothels during the previous two years in Bristol, Weston-Super-Mare and Cheltenham. We had briefed his legal advisor with the mass of evidence against his client and when we went in to interview Anthony Gough, he admitted the offences fully. He claimed that he had opened the brothels to help get the prostitutes off the street and to work in a safer environment. He claimed not to have made a substantial amount of money from the businesses. He accepted that he had rented the two properties in Cheltenham, in Evesham Road and Clarence Road, rented two houses in Filton Avenue, Bristol, rented a house in Walliscote Road Weston-Super-Mare and rented a property in Soundwell Road. The prostitutes used where all willing participants and none were working under duress. He took what he considered as a reasonable cut from the girls' earnings as the rent had to be paid, the advertising cost money and he had purchased phones for the addresses so he could help if any clients caused problems. Anthony Gough was charged and bailed to attend court with conditions not to contact any of the prostitutes.

Anthony Gough later pleaded guilty in court and was sentenced to 18 months in prison suspended for 2 years.

You may think that is the end of this story but there is a little more to tell you about what happened to Celia, Debbie, and Louise.

At 7:45pm on Tuesday 29th August 2000, Detective Constable Rob Calloway answered a call in the office from Celia Black. She sounded in an angry stressed state and was screaming down the phone that she had been robbed and wanted the CID to attend and deal with it. I decided to go with Rob to Celia's work address in Rush Close, Bradley Stoke, Bristol. Celia reported that since leaving

90

Soundwell Road she had decided to continue the brothel business with Louise Brown and Debbie Johnson but with no man running things, so all the earning were shared out between the three of them after costs. The premises was right in the middle of a large residential estate so was likely to attract complaints from neighbours. They had only been there about one month but were already well established and the house had a cleaner and more professional look about it than the other brothels I had seen.

Celia explained that she had taken a call from a prospective client and was expecting him to arrive when the front doorbell rang. She answered the door to two men with their lower face covered in scarves. One was brandishing a 4" knife. The man was shouting:

"Give us your money, we know you must have money, you've been working all day".

Celia handed over all the daily takings from a cash box in the lounge. It was about £1,500. The two lads then ran off. Celia was convinced that Anthony Gough was behind the robbery because she had recognised the man without the knife as Richard Forrest a close friend of Gough and Richard's friend with the knife was Joe McGuire.

Having carried out our own research, at 11:40am the following day Rob and I went to Forrest's home address in Little Stoke, Bristol and as we arrived, we saw two men leaving the property from the rear door. The two fitted the description of the robbers, given by Celia the previous day. Rob approached Forrest to arrest him, and then took him back inside the house to search for the knife. I approached the second lad, Joe McGuire and said:

"Joe, I am arresting you on suspicion of a robbery which occurred yesterday afternoon at an address in Rush Close, Bradley Stoke. You have been named as one of the people involved".

After caution he said:

"Yeah OK".

I told McGuire that as he lived nearby, we would be searching his house next as we were looking for certain clothing and a knife. McGuire said that the knife was not at his house but in a friend's car and he would direct us there to recover it. I told him to say nothing more until he was interviewed on tape. But he said:

"You know what those ladies do".

Before heading to the station with Forrest and McGuire, we stopped to recover the knife from an insecure car parked nearby and we also recovered McGuire's scarf from his home address.

The two lads were interviewed under caution at the police station and they both admitted the robbery stating that they had stolen £1650 in cash from the prostitute's house in Bradley Stoke. They had done it to pay off a debt to someone who had told them about the brothel and had suggested that the girls would never report the robbery because of the business they were in. They refused to name the person but when asked the direct question they admitted to knowing Anthony Gough, who they used to run errands for.

Forrest and McGuire were charged with robbery and pleaded guilty at court. Both received suspended sentences. There was never enough evidence to link Anthony Gough to the robbery.

The next case is not really the type of offence that a vice detective would be allocated to investigate. It does not involve prostitution, controlled drugs, or illegal alcohol. This case is more about the offender's personal vice. A vice being defined as an immoral or wicked personal characteristic. It does involve non-consensual sex and gives you an idea of the diverse cases I dealt with during my police service.

Chapter 3:

Lucy

At 8:00am on a Saturday morning in July 2000, I was working out of Staplehill Police station as a Detective Sergeant when I received a call to attend a serious sexual assault at Homelands Cottage in Winterbourne. It was only a 15-minute journey away and as I arrived, I was greeted by PC Davies, the first uniform officer who had attended. The officer went on to explain that the witness Mr Jones had been asleep in bed when at about 2:30am in the morning, he was awoken by a terrible commotion coming from one of the outhouses in his small homestead. He went out to the building and discovered Lucy, she was tied to a wooden pillar with ropes around her legs and neck. Mr Jones described himself as Lucy's carer and having untied her, he took her to much warmer comfortable surroundings, in a hope this would calm her down. When I met her, it was obvious that Lucy was deeply traumatised by whatever had happened to her. You could see the terror in her eyes and obvious panic. We would not be able to get any account from her about what had occurred, that was quite clear. PC Davies explained that this was the second Saturday running that Lucy had been attacked in the same way which was why he had requested the attendance of a Detective Sergeant.

There was very little evidence to be discovered in the outhouse, there was the remains of the rope used to tie her up, this had been brought to the scene by the attacker. It was quite standard rope, a thick blue twine in several pieces that had originally been over 4m in length and could easily be bought in local DIY stores. The rope was seized in a hope that the offender's DNA might be found on it, deposited when he pulled it tight to tie the knots. There was a large cushion that had been dragged by the offender into the outhouse possibly to provide comfort for him when carrying out his attack. I decided that our best chances of getting the offender's DNA would be to arrange a medical examination of Lucy which Mr Jones agreed to as Lucy was unable to consent herself. The medical examination was carried out by Dr Easton who recorded injuries to the genital area. Several intimate swabs were taken, and I took possession of these to submit to forensic scientists for analysis.

I decided that, as Lucy had clearly been targeted as a victim, I would rush through the forensic submissions in a hope of identifying the offender. The forensic results were back within 48 hours and semen had been detected on the vaginal swabs. The semen had produced a full male DNA profile of the attacker, but the bad news was that no DNA hit had been obtained from the national DNA database. The offender had not previously had his DNA taken.

I got agreement from senior management that we needed to act in case the offender should attempt a third attack on the following Saturday and so I planned a sting operation. There were some risks with the sting operation because Lucy would in effect be the bait for the attacker and we were unhappy with putting her at risk again. The attacker would need to be caught virtually in the act of committing the crime as simply finding him in the cottage grounds would be a civil trespass offence and not sufficient to prove a sexual assault.

Mr Jones took some persuading but once he was assured that enough safeguards were in place he agreed.

By midnight on the following Friday night, four officers and I were hiding in strategic locations on the outskirts of Homelands Cottage, there was also a dog handler, Ray Holmes and his faithful dog Sabre sat in a police van further down the lane. We had the police IT department set up movement sensors in the fields close to the cottage and contact sensors placed on the entrance gate so hopefully we should get some early notification of an offender's approach. The location was quite remote in an isolated lane in the countryside.

As 2:30 arrived, it was deadly silent when suddenly one of the movement sensors was activated. We had been warned that badgers, foxes and alike would also activate the sensors so we needed to wait for further confirmation. Staring out into the night, DC

Meadows could make out the silhouette of a man dressed all in black, walking slowly towards the property. The man was lost to sight briefly, but the gate contact sensor sounded in our ears and we knew precisely where the man must be. It was still too early to call the strike; it had been agreed at the briefing that 2 minutes after the gate was opened the strike would be called. This should give the attacker time to get into the outbuilding and prepare it for his intended attack as he had done on the two previous occasions. It was the longest 2 minutes I think I have experienced but I shouted *"Strike, Strike, Strike"* as soon as two minutes had passed. We all ran towards the cottage but as we were approaching the gate, we could see the man running full pelt, leaping a fence, and heading out across the fields. Ray released Sabre who set off in hot pursuit and Sabre was soon making ground. The man dived into some bushes followed immediately by Sabre and Ray was some 50 metres away. As Ray got to the hedge, he could hear shouts and screams coming from the bushes and called for Sabre to leave. The man was happy to be arrested as the dog was now under the control of his handler.

Two of the team had headed straight for the outhouse as had been planned in the briefing but once they entered, they were shocked to find that Lucy was stood there, tied by the neck and legs to the same wooden pole, looking very shaken and confused.

The offender may have been caught but the fact that Lucy had been put through, yet another horrific ordeal made you wonder if it was all worth it.

The offender was taken to Staplehill police station where he was placed in a cell. It was necessary to arrange for an interpreter for his interview as he was a Hungarian national.

Stefan Janos was a 35-year-old Hungarian male who was a married man with two children. He had been brought up in Hungary by his parents and had two brothers and 3 sisters. The family had lived a nomadic life, constantly on the move and travelling from place to place in horse drawn caravans.

At the age of 17, he left Hungary and travelled alone to England where he had lived ever since. I have little doubt that his English was perfect, but he insisted that he required an interpreter because of the nature of the allegations.

Detective Constable Russ Jones from our CID office carried out the interviews with a Hungarian interpreter. Stefan could not accept that he had done anything wrong even though he accepted that he was the person responsible for taking Lucy to the outhouse on the previous two weeks. He had always been taught by his father that behaving in the manner he had was quite acceptable and enjoyable to both parties. A DNA swab was taken from him and later confirmed that it was him who had sexual contact with Lucy, but he would never explain the full extent of the assault and Lucy was never able to give her account.

Stefan was charged with bestiality and sentenced to 6 months imprisonment, I have no idea what he told his wife or family about his offences.

If you have not already worked it out, Lucy was a 5-year-old horse. It took her six months before she started trusting men again. We have no idea of the long-term effect it had on her but hopefully from that day on she led a happier life.

Greed

Chapter 1:

Funny Money

Counterfeit money is defined as currency that is produced without the legal sanction of the government to resemble official currency closely enough that it may be confused for genuine currency. Producing or using counterfeit money is a form of fraud.

The main offences in relation to counterfeit currency are:

- Any person making a counterfeit of a currency note or of a protected coin, intending that they or another shall pass or tender it as genuine.

- For a person to pass or tender as genuine anything which is, or which they know or believe to be, a counterfeit of a currency note or of a protected coin.

- To deliver to another anything which is, or which they know or believe to be, such a counterfeit, intending that the person to whom it is delivered or another shall pass or tender it as genuine.

The maximum sentence for tendering counterfeit money is **ten years imprisonment**.

It was a Thursday evening in late March 1999 I was sat at home enjoying a quiet evening with my family. At 7:00pm the phone rang and I immediately recognised the cheery voice of Detective Constable (Himey) Hieron. I could hear the excitement in his voice as he went on to explain how he had just received a phone call from a casual informant David Deacon who he had not spoken to for over a year.

David was a 35-year-old single man who was unemployed but tended to take on any cash in hand work he could find. He also liked to be a paid informant to subsidise his income whenever necessary. David was a petty criminal in his own right and had a reputation of handling stolen goods and being able to get hold of anything you needed by either legitimate or illegal means. David had phoned Himey because earlier that evening he had been drinking in his local pub in the Lawrence Hill area of Bristol when an acquaintance of his had introduced him to two men, Martin and Paul. The two men had a proposition for him regarding counterfeit money. They handed David a forged £20 note and stated they were looking for someone who was able to take large quantities of forged currency and get it into general circulation without raising suspicion. The men claimed to be part of an organised gang that were from out of Bristol and who had the ability to print vast quantities of counterfeit currency but were not interested dealing in only small amounts. David had looked at the £20 note and was really impressed at the quality of it. The printing was clear, there was an apparent watermark and a strip through the note and when he compared it to the genuine article, he couldn't tell them apart. Martin handed him another nine £20 notes, all forgeries and David was surprised to see that they all had different serial numbers. David agreed that if he could keep the notes, he had some ideas where he may be able to find people who could take regular large amounts to feed into circulation. Martin and Paul agreed and exchanged mobile phone numbers with David so he could contact them once a distributor had been found. Martin who had done most of the talking said David could keep the ten notes as a sample. He stated that they were only printing £20 notes at that moment in time but could branch out more if business improved.

I have little doubt that David could have identified people who would have been willing to purchase forged notes at a knock down price but he had other plans on this occasion. David saw this as an opportunity to get a reasonable informant pay-out with no risk of arrest and it was for that reason, he had phoned Himey. David wanted to meet up with Himey to pass over the information.

I told Himey to arrange a meeting with David that evening at 9:00pm and we would take things from there dependant on what facts we could glean from David. I pointed out that for Himey's own protection I would also attend the meeting with him so asked that he identify a location and we would meet up beforehand at St George Police station to collect a car and plan our strategy.

By 8:50pm Himey and I were sat in a quiet industrial estate awaiting David's arrival. We were deliberately 10 minutes early for the meeting as we wanted to make sure that David arrived alone and there was no trap being set for us. David in fact arrived ten minutes late but he arrived alone and approached the car and tapped on the front passenger window where Himey was sat. Himey told him to sit in the rear of the car so that we could talk. The location chosen by Himey was excellent as we saw no-one during the half hour we sat there chatting.

David repeated the information that he had supplied Himey over the telephone. He only had the first names of the two men offering the forged currency those being Martin and Paul. David gave detailed descriptions of them including the fact that they had Geordie accents. He supplied us with the phone number that Martin had given him and he also supplied us with the name of his acquaintance who had first introduced the men to him. David explained that the men were hoping to deal in thousands of pounds worth of currency at a time and the larger the quantity the better rate of profit he could make.

David reached into the inside breast pocket of his coat and produced a white plain oblong envelope which he said contained £200 worth of the forged currency in 10 X £20 notes. Himey and I had come prepared and put on latex gloves before we took possession of the envelope. We counted the notes and certainly agreed that they looked like the real thing and would fool most people. The envelope was David's so had no importance to us as it had not been handled by the suspects. Himey placed the notes into a numbered self-seal clear bag and wrote out a receipt, which David signed. I should point out that the name David Deacon was his 'informant' name used whenever he gave information or contacted Himey. He used that name to sign the receipt. David's real name was only known by very few people to protect him from being identified. David as you might expect did not want a copy of the receipt as he could not afford to be found with it.

We explained that we would carry out further inquiries into the information that he had supplied and would come up with a plan how to identify and arrest suspects without compromising David in any way. David was told that should his information result in the arrest of Martin, Paul or other gang members for offences of counterfeiting he would be paid handsomely for his information.

On Friday morning I sat down with Himey to formulate a plan of investigation and decide who would be best placed to continue the enquiry. It is quite normal for the officer handling the informant not to be the one conducting the investigation as this can lead to difficulties when the investigating officer is cross examined in court. If the investigating officer truly had no idea who the informant in a case is then they will find answering questions under cross examination much easier and not appear evasive in the witness box.

We first wanted to know before we handed things over if we could confirm that the notes were in fact counterfeit. This question was answered quite quickly but even the experts were surprised by the excellent quality of the forgeries. They were able to also confirm that other similar currency was circulating around the Newcastle area and in London.

There were certain enquiries that we could make at this time in an attempt to identify the people involved. We had a phone number used by Martin but enquiries into that number showed no registered user. How the user of the phone paid for calls etc would take much longer to establish and that enquiry would be left to others to carry out. We had the 10 x £20 notes, which if our understanding was correct, had not been in previous general circulation and were quite fresh in appearance. It was likely that very few people had handled the notes since they were printed so there was a reasonable possibility that if any fingerprints were found they could belong to suspects. David Deacon's prints would have to be eliminated first but this was a reasonable line of investigation for us to do at this stage.

We had the name of David's associate who introduced Martin and Paul to him so we carried out research on him in a hope of identifying anyone that fitted the description given of Martin and Paul.

Within a few days it was clear that no fingerprint identification was going to happen and no intelligence checks would give us the identities of Martin, Paul or other gang members.

Having consulted with the Detective Inspector and due to the fact that the criminals appeared to be active in Newcastle and London as well as Bristol, it was agreed that the National Crime Squad should be contacted for them to further the investigation. Himey submitted a lengthy report and then we had to sit and await the response.

It was about one week later when the National Crime Squad made contact with us requesting a meeting to discuss the information and their plans for catching the offenders. We met at an unspecified location and were all sat around a large desk. The crime squad supervisor explained that he agreed that the information looked genuine and there was a clear opportunity to close down a serious crime group's operation regarding widespread counterfeit currency. They stated that other information pointed towards an organised crime group based in Liverpool being responsible so relished the challenge. Their plan was for our informant to initially be introduced to an undercover police officer, who was from another police area not connected to Bristol, London, Newcastle or Liverpool. The officer was an Asian male of Indian origin aged about 28 years old going by the name of Tony Sidhu. His story was that his family owned a number of shops in the Birmingham and Bristol areas and as the result, were able to launder a large quantity of the forged notes through their businesses without raising any suspicion. If he agreed, all David would be required to do was to introduce Tony Sidhu to Martin and Paul and then have no further contact with any of them.

Tony Sidhu would gain the trust of the suppliers and put in an initial order for a quantity of forged notes. If everything went smoothly for both the suppliers and Tony, he would agree to follow up with regular orders. The plan appeared quite simple and had a level of protection for David keeping him away from the offenders when arrests were planned for the future. Arrests were to be on a much later date and there were discussions that even Tony Sidhu might be arrested to protect the source of the information.

Himey made contact with David Deacon and gave him a very brief outline of the plan as had been agreed by the crime squad supervisor. David agreed that he would make the introductions and was happy not to be involved any further. Himey and I took David up to the Bristol Downs where, near the sea walls we met up with Tony Sidhu. He appeared to fit the role and came across as very convincing. We introduced David to Tony but obviously using David's true name as that was the name Martin

108

and Paul knew him by. We only ever knew Tony by his undercover name and this was the one and only time we were to meet him. Himey and I left David and Tony to discuss the plans together and once they had finished, we took David back to the St George area of Bristol so he could carry on his day. Himey and I were not privy to any more details as to when or where the undercover cover officer was to be taken to speak with Martin and Paul.

It was only about two weeks later when Himey received a phone call from David Deacon who was not at all pleased with the way things had progressed. David explained that he had introduced Tony to Martin and Paul at his local pub. The three appeared to get along well and David had left them to discuss the business dealings together. David had heard about three days later that everything had fallen through with the deal because Tony had requested to put in an order for £1,000,000 worth of counterfeit notes. Such a huge order made the gang too suspicious so they severed ties with Tony immediately. I often use the term 'softly, softly, catchy monkey' and I have no idea why the crime squad had decided to start with such a large amount of cash rather than a more reasonable £10,000 order. I'm sure had they not been so greedy and so impatient they may well have had successful arrests and prosecutions.

What annoyed David most was the fact that he was not paid any money for the information he had supplied as no arrests were made.

Preview of other books in the series

If you enjoyed reading 'The Vice Detective' then you may also be interested in the other books in the series written by me. 'The Murder Detective' and 'The Cold Case Detective'.

The Murder Detective:

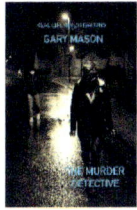

Follows me on three different murder cases and a manslaughter investigation during my years in the Avon and Somerset Police. They are only a few of the murders that I have worked on, but each was in a different role and are fascinating for different reasons.

The first case is the murder of shopkeeper Roy Page in 1985. Roy was running a sweetshop in St John Lane, Bedminster, Bristol, when a mysterious man purporting to be a gas board official called at his shop and beat him to death. I was called in on day 1 to carry out Exhibit Officer duties for the investigation and I also sat through the trial as the investigation reached its conclusion. The case shows the power of the media and the public, who between them, identified the offender and directed the police to arrest the man. It details the bizarre account given by the offender to avoid conviction.

The second case was in 1998 and I will lead you through the investigation into the murder of Jenny King, a 22-year-old girl, who was attacked and murdered whilst walking home from a night club in Kingswood, Bristol. I was on duty at Staplehill CID when Jenny King was reported as a missing person and I was then working in the incident room and was the case officer throughout the trial. You will learn about the recovery of a vast amount of evidence and how several experts were able to prove the case against Paul Hunt as well as how evidence nearly pointed towards two innocent men.

The third case is the murder of Patrick Logan in 2000 during a robbery at his home in Castlejordan, Co Meath, Ireland. I will detail how Detective Constable Ian Hieron and I worked closely with the Garda using our initiative and untried methods, recovered important evidence that enabled the Garda to arrest the offenders for the murder and secure convictions.

The manslaughter tells the tragic tale surrounding the accidental death of a university student in 1992. The battles to prove the gross negligence of the people culpable for his death, in order for his family to feel that someone was being held responsible for the incident and to prevent future deaths in similar circumstances.

The final two cases in this book look at the specific crime described as domestic homicide. I look at a male and female victim who were ferociously attacked. The similar defences put forward by the suspects and the different outcomes on the cases.

The Cold Case Detective:

Follows me working on nine different stranger rape cold case offences during my years in the Avon and Somerset Police. They are only a few of the many cases that I have worked on, but each was different and are fascinating for different reasons.

The rape offences date from 1979 up to 1992 and with the help of forensic science specifically DNA, 6 different offenders are brought to justice. The Cold Case Unit started in 2003 and the investigations all resulted in convictions. I worked on the unit until my retirement in 2020.

The final story is a cold case murder investigation. Melanie Road was walking home alone in Bath in 1984 when she was stabbed to death and sexually assaulted. Her attacker remained free to live his life until 2015, when due to incredible determination and persistence by the police officers involved, Melanie's attacker was arrested. Read how he was identified and the efforts put in to prove his guilt.

Dedication

I would like to dedicate this story to all the brave and courageous victims. They have dealt with so much during the initial assaults and the re-investigations. It is their determination for justice that kept my motivation and drive for relentlessly pursuing the offenders. The police and forensic scientists do their jobs to help victims move forward in their lives, I wish the results could be immediate. I continued to hunt down these evil offenders until my retirement in 2020 and then passed on the work to other investigators.

I would like to thank my niece Camille Leveau for her photographic skills in producing the superb book covers and I wish her well in her future in photography.

I must mention my friend Robert Murphy who is a well-respected journalist who I met many times during my career and who has reported on a number of these cases over the years. It was Robert who encouraged me to write this book and has given me support and guidance throughout.

I would also like to make mention of the three ladies in my life, Bernie, my wife and my two daughters Blandine and Chloe. There were many occasions during my 43 years police service when I was absent from home due to working overtime or cancelled rest days. I hope by reading this story they will understand the reasons for my absences. I would never have had the energy and fighting spirit if they had not been so supportive. I also hope that my grandsons Luca, Marco, Renzo, Jacob and Oscar get a chance to read the story when they are older. I would love them to understand the work that their Papu did in the police.

Gary Mason

About the author

I joined the Avon and Somerset police in March 1977 and was posted as a uniform constable to 'B' Division working predominantly on the Knowle West council estate. I was a prolific thief taker and this resulted in me being successful in my application to become a detective constable based at Bishopsworth Police station in 1983. Between 1983 and 1989 I learnt my trade in crime investigation and was involved in several high-profile investigations. In 1985 I got my first taste of murder investigations when I was the exhibits officer in the investigation into the murder of shop owner Royston Page in Bedminster, Bristol. The case was detected with the help of the media (Crimewatch UK) when an appeal was put out to identify a bogus gas official seen in the area at the time of the murder. I carried out duties in the role of an acting sergeant on the CID until my eventual promotion in 1989. For one-year, I again performed uniform duties as a sergeant covering the St Pauls area of Bristol. Drugs and prostitution were the main social problems that the police were required to deal with. The draw of crime investigation was too much and I jumped at the opportunity to return to CID work in 1990 and was posted to Yeovil CID office. The daily travel from Bristol to Yeovil for a whole year proved too much and I was not seeing enough of my family, my wife Bernadette and daughters Blandine and Chloe. I requested to return to Bristol. Between 1991 and 2002, I worked at various CID offices around Bristol, Redland, Southmead, St George and Staplehill and took any opportunity to be seconded to murder investigations where I felt I got the greatest satisfaction. I trained as a scene liaison officer attending murder crime scenes and post-mortems and I became well known for working in major incident rooms using the HOLMES computerised recording system. In October 1998, I was the receiver and case supervisor in one of the Avon and Somerset's largest and most well-known murder investigation, the murder of 22-year-old Jenny King as she walked home from a night club in Kingswood, Bristol. This investigation stirred up a media frenzy which continued until the eventual conviction of Paul Hunt in March 2000. In 2002 the Avon and Somerset police set up a dedicated Major Crime Investigation Unit to investigate all murders in the force area and I was one of 4 detective sergeants selected to be part of this unit. In 2003 the Major Crime Investigation Unit were tasked with setting up a cold case investigation section and I took the lead role in forming a small group of officers and staff to investigate cold case stranger rape offences. I remained working on the MCIU until my retirement after 31 years service in February 2008. With only 2 weeks off, I commenced employment as a crime investigator with the Avon and Somerset police working in their Major Crime Review Team.   The MCRT provide support and guidance to senior investigating officers in undetected murders and stranger rape offences and also took on the responsibility of cold case investigations. At the time of writing, I am no longer employed with the police having retired in 2020 after a total of 43 years service. The book contains only a very small number of complex investigations that I worked on.

Printed in Great Britain
by Amazon

45658160R00066